ESCAPE

True Accounts of POW Escapes

G. S. Willmott

Willmott G S
Title: Escape - True Accounts of POW Escapes / Garry Willmott.

Revised edition.
ISBN: 9781925280791 (paperback)
ISBN: 9781925280807 (eBook)

Military History

Published by Crabtree Pty Ltd

Digital editions distributed by
Port Campbell Press

Table of Contents

Introduction

Wars are usually fought over territory, natural resources or religious differences whatever the reason they have created, changed or destroyed entire nations. The oldest profession in the world is the military the second oldest profession followed the armies on their conquests. War reaches back to the beginning of mankind although the first recorded war occurred in 2700 B.C. The belligerents were Sumer (in modern Iraq) and Elam (a region that is now part of Iran) This conflict was fought in the area around Basra in Iraq. Of course, tribes, cities, etc., had been fighting each other for thousands of years before that, but there are no written records of these earlier conflicts.

Prisoners of War (POW) helped establish and build nations such as Egypt, Rome, Athens and the Persian Empire. All these nations and cities rose or fell on the strength of their armies.

The dictionary definition of Prisoner of War is:

"A prisoner of war (POW) enemy prisoner of war (EPW) or Missing-Captured is a person, whether combatant or non-combatant, who is held in custody by an enemy power during or immediately after an armed conflict."

The earliest recorded usage of the phrase is dated 1660.

For most of human history depending on the culture of the victors, combatants on the losing side in a battle could expect to be either slaughtered or enslaved.

The first Roman gladiators were prisoners of war and were named according to their ethnic roots such as Samnite, Thracian and the Gaul. Homer's Iliad describes Greek and Trojan soldiers offering rewards of wealth to enemies who have defeated them on the battlefield in exchange for mercy, their offers were not always accepted.

In the later Middle Ages, a number of religious wars aimed to not only defeat but also eliminate their enemies. In Christian Europe, the extermination of the heretics or "non-believers" was considered their main objective. Examples include the 13th century Albigensian Crusade and the Northern Crusades. When asked by a Crusader how to distinguish between the Catholics and Cathars once they'd taken the city of Béziers, the Papal Legate Arnaud Amalric famously replied, "Kill them all, God will know His own".

Likewise the inhabitants of conquered cities were frequently massacred during the Crusades against the Muslims in the 11th and 12th centuries. Noblemen could hope to be ransomed; their families would have to send to their captors large sums of money depending on their social status.

Many French prisoners of war were killed during the Battle of Agincourt in 1415

In feudal Japan there was no custom for ransoming prisoners of war, who were for the most part summarily executed

Every city or town that refused surrender and resisted the Mongols was subject to destruction

The Aztecs were constantly at war with neighbouring tribes and groups. The goal of this constant warfare was to collect live prisoners for sacrifice.

In pre-Islamic Arabia, upon capture, those captives not executed were made to beg for their subsistence. During the early reforms under Islam, Muhammad changed this custom and made it the responsibility of the Islamic government to provide food and clothing on a reasonable basis to captives, regardless of their religion.

The freeing of prisoners in particular was highly recommended as a charitable act. Christians, who were captured during the Crusades, were usually either killed or sold into slavery if they could not pay a ransom.

After the Napoleonic wars between 1796 and 1797 a camp was built at Norman Cross near Peterborough in England to accommodate seven thousand French prisoners of war. This was the first purpose built POW camp; it was situated on a forty-acre tract of land. London was only 78 miles to the south by the Great North Road.

So began the era of escape.

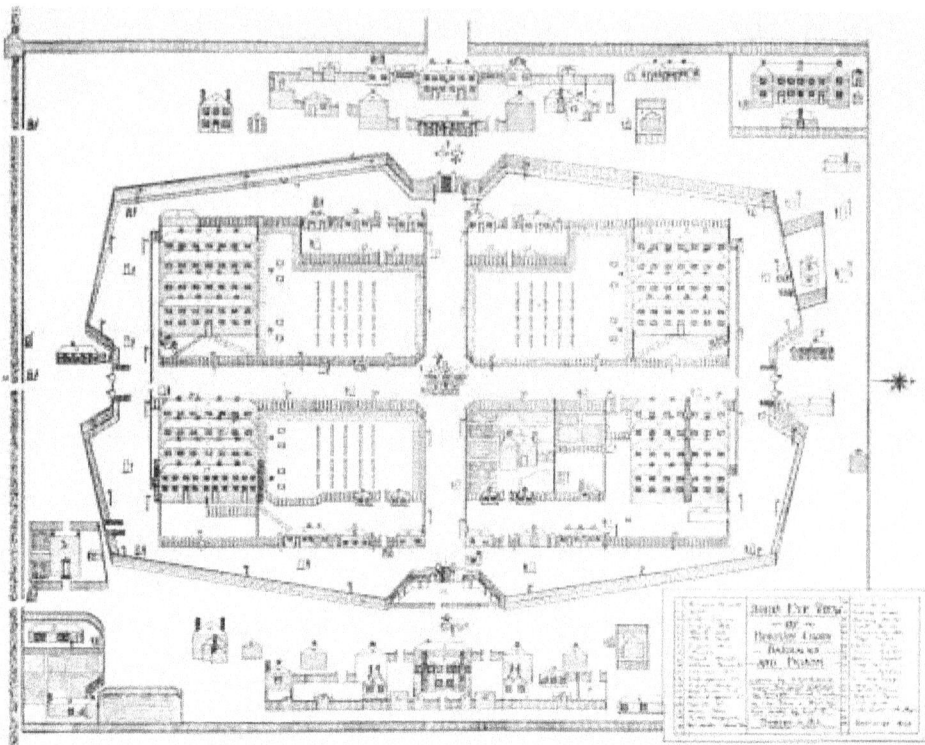

PLAN D.—BIRD'S-EYE VIEW OF NORMAN CROSS BARRACKS AND PRISON, EAST ELEVATION.
Executed by Lieutenant E. Macgregor, 1813.

Six prisoners escaped in April 1801. Three of them were caught at Boston, Lincolnshire and the remaining three were caught in a fishing boat off the Norfolk coast.

Three groups of 16 men each escaped in late 1801.

Incomplete tunnels were discovered in 1802.

After two major escape attempts in 1804 and 1807, the wooden stockade fence was replaced with a brick wall

One prisoner, Charles Francois Bourchier, stabbed a civilian Alexander Halliday while attempting to escape on 9 September 1808.

6

He was convicted at the Huntingdon Assizes and sentenced to death by hanging. He was executed at the prison in front of the prisoners and the whole garrison

After the stabbing, the entire prison was searched and seven hundred daggers were found

In January 1812, a French prisoner was shot whilst escaping after he had overpowered a guard and stolen a bayonet.

"Escape" follows the adventures of some incredibly brave intelligent and determined men and women.

What drives a prisoner to risk punishment and sometimes death to escape from their captors and return home to their mother country only to re-enter the conflict putting their lives on the line once more.

Many POWs behaved themselves and as a result were treated reasonably with three meals a day, exercise and plenty of reading material. The Red Cross parcels supplied them with little luxuries like tobacco and chocolate. Officers were allowed beer and wine with their evening meal.

Those who chose to escape had a burning desire to rejoin the war and continue to serve their country.

We follow the adventures of Gunter Pluschow a German aviator who escaped Tsing-tao a German post in China after it had been taken by the English and Japanese. His route took him to Japan, the United States and Gibraltar before being captured and interred in several POW camps in England. He was the first and only German to escape from an English camp in World War One.

On the opposing side William Leefe Robinson the first aviator to shoot down a German Zeppelin. He received a Victoria Cross for his gallantry. He was shot down over France and captured by the Germans. His treatment in the German camps including Colditz was atrocious.

The first American to escape from a German camp was Frank Zavicki a young Polish immigrant. His escape is quite amazing.

Horace Greasley a British soldier holds the record for the number of successful escapes, two hundred! Why? His lover Rosa would be able to answer that.

'Escape" also follows escapes from camps such as Holzminden, Colditz and Auschwitz.

While the human race exists there will be war, I wish that was not the case but the reality is John Lennon's legendry song "Imagine" is a fantasy.

While war exists there will be Prisoners of War. While POWs exist there will be escapes.

Civil Unrest

Chapter 1

At the outbreak of the Civil War in 1861, Luther Libby was running a ship supply store from the corner of a large warehouse in Richmond, Virginia. The building had been used as a tobacco factory prior to Libby taking possession. In need of a new prison for captured Union officers, the Confederate Government gave Libby 48 hours to evacuate his property. The sign over the northwest corner reading "L. Libby & Son, Ship Chandlers" was never removed, and consequently the building and prison bore his name. Since the Confederates believed the building was escape proof, the prison guards considered their job relatively straightforward.

Most people around the globe have assumed the Civil War occurred because the North was no longer willing to tolerate slavery as being part of the structure of U.S. society and that the political power brokers in Washington were planning to abolish slavery throughout the Union. Therefore, for most people, slavery was the fundamental issue in explaining the causes of the American Civil War.

It's not quite that simple; slavery was a major issue but not the only factor in pushing America into a horrendous bloody conflict.

By April 1861 the slavery issue had been entwined with other major issues such as state rights. The southern states objected to the fact that the Federal Government was dictating what was wrong and what was right. These southerners felt their whole way of life was changing for the worse and they didn't like it.

All these issues contributed to the American Civil War.

By 1860 America could not be seen as one society. The North and the South were like two separate counties, each with their own value systems and interpretation of the rule of law.

It became North versus South, The Union versus The Confederates: WAR.

The South was agrarian; cotton and tobacco were the main backbone to the region's economic strength. The southern states relied on exports to markets in Western Europe. The class structure in Britain was mimicked in the south. The local plantation owner was a 'Baron' within his own domain; the local population would be deferential towards such men. The South constituted a strictly Christian society that had a hierarchy of men at the top while those underneath were expected and required to accept their social status. Social advancement for the less privileged was possible but unusual; invariably one advanced within the senior families who were the economic, political and legal brokers of their state.

Certainly the wealth created by the plantation owners relied heavily on slave labour and was accepted in the south as the natural way of doing things.

If slave labour were no longer available to them their wealth would have been seriously affected. It was not only the barons who would suffer but also the local communities that relied on their support would have suffered.

When the dogs of war began to howl in 1860-61, many in the South saw their very way of life being threatened. Part of that included slavery, but it was not the only part.

The North's way of life was diametrically opposed to the South; it had become an industrial powerhouse and was growing at an incredible pace.

In the North you did not need to be born into a wealthy family. Many poor boys became entrepreneurs, such as Samuel Colt who died a multi-millionaire.

Cornelius Vanderbilt was another example. Whether an immigrant from the Netherlands could have made his way into the social hierarchy of the South is open to debate. The North was also a cosmopolitan mixture of nationalities and religions – far more so than the South. There can be little doubt that there were important groups in the North that were anti-slavery and wanted its abolition throughout the Union. However, there were also groups that were ambivalent and those who knew that the North's economic development was based not only on entrepreneurial skills but also on the input of poorly paid workers who were not slaves but lived lives not totally removed from those in the South. While they had their freedom and were paid, their lifestyle was at best very harsh.

While the belligerents of the American Civil War were opposed in many areas, it became worse with the perception in the South that the North would try to impose its own values on their beloved land.

In 1832, South Carolina passed an act declaring Federal tariff legislation could not be enforced onto states. This meant after February 1st 1833 the tariffs would not be recognised in South Carolina. This brought the rogue State into direct conflict with the Federal government in Washington DC.

Congress passed the "Force Bill" enabling the President to use military force to bring any state into line with regards to implementing Federal law. On this occasion the threat of military force worked, South Carolina capitulated.

It was at this time slavery became entwined with state rights. The question was: how much power had a state compared to Federal authority? The key issue was whether slavery would be allowed to continue in the newly created States that were joining the Union?

This dispute escalated when the federal government purchased Kansas. The new state was officially opened for settlement in 1854, when both pro-slavery and anti-slavery settlers poured in, setting up a scenario of violence and acrimony.

On January 29th 1861, Kansas was admitted to the Union as a slave-free state. Many in the traditional slave states of the South saw this as the first step towards abolishing slavery throughout the Union and thus the destruction of their southern way of life.

South Carolina seceded from the Union on December 20th 1860, the first state to do so; it felt it was being dominated by a Federal Government, which was controlled by the North. Whether this was true or not, is not relevant as it was felt to be true by many South Carolinians. The secession of South Carolina pushed other southern states into doing the same. With such a background of distrust between most southern states and the Government in Washington, it only needed one incident to set off a civil war and that occurred at Fort Sumter in April 1861.

Fort Sumter

The attack on Fort Sumter began on Friday, April 12th, 1861. It is seen as the start of the American Civil War.

In 1860, a Federal grant of $80,000 was given to complete the construction of Fort Sumter, as it had lain unfinished for a number of years.

The fort was constructed to hold a garrison of 650 men.

On 12 April 1861, General P.G.T. Beauregard of the Confederate forces attacked Fort Sumter. The fort housed three 10-inch guns placed to cover all the important angles. The fort also housed 8-inch columbiads, 42lbs, 32lbs and 24lbs guns and some 8-inch sea howitzers. Fort Sumter had its own fresh water supply and a hospital.

All hell was about to break loose: 625,000 people would lose their lives, many of them children.

Union Columbiad

It was not fully manned when it was attacked but still held out until April 22nd after more than 40,000 shells had been fired at her.

By the end of the war in 1865, Fort Sumter was little more than a pile of rubble after constant shelling by Union forces.

The Great Union Escape

Libby Prison

The Libby Prison Escape at Richmond, Virginia, in February 1864 saw over one hundred Union prisoners-of-war escape from captivity. It was one of the most successful prison breaks of the American Civil War.

Led by Colonel Thomas E. Rose of the 77th Pennsylvania Infantry, the prisoners started tunnelling in a rat-infested area, which the Confederate guards were reluctant to enter. The tunnel emerged in a vacant lot beside a warehouse, from where the escapees could walk out through the gate without arousing suspicion. Since the prison was believed to be escape-proof, there was less vigilance by the authorities than in other camps, and the alarm was not raised for nearly twelve hours. Over half the prisoners were able to reach Union lines.

The complex was converted to a prison in March 1862 in response to problems at a prisoner depot in central Richmond. Located at Main and 25th streets, this facility had been established in 1861 after the first Union prisoners began pouring into Richmond following the First Battle of Manassas on July 21. Its location made it difficult to secure, Confederate officials decided to occupy the Libby buildings because they were more secure. As the number of Union prisoners increased after the Seven Day Battles in June 1862, Libby Prison could not cope with the numbers and was therefore designated an officers-only facility.

Connected by thick inner doors, the three Libby buildings came to be known as East, Middle, and West. The Union POWs were confined to the upper two floors, which contained six sparsely furnished rooms; there were no bunks and few benches and each measured 105 by 45 feet. Wooden bars covered small windows, which offered no protection from the steaming heat in summer or bitter cold in winter. Little light permeated through these windows, making the cells a very dark inhospitable environment to live in. The kitchen was located on the first floor, Middle, and was the only room to which inmates had free access. The hospital was on the first floor, East, with offices and guardrooms on the first floor, West. The cellar was reserved for a carpenter shop and slave accommodation. The centre cellar had four solitary confinement cells reserved for troublemakers.

Escape from Libby Prison

In late 1863, a group of Union officers began making plans to escape from the Confederate prison. They removed a stove located on the first floor and began digging their way into the adjoining building's chimney. The intending escapees constructed a tight but usable passage for access to the eastern basement. Having gained access to the basement, it was determined that a tunnel could be dug to Kerr's Warehouse to the east. From there they could escape into the street.

The escapees divided themselves into three digging squads comprising five men each. Using a broken shovel and two knives stolen from the kitchen for tools they began their endeavour. Most of their digging took place at night, as the Confederate guards were more likely to notice prisoners missing during daylight hours.

Digging the tunnel was not an easy task. Not only were they in complete darkness but the air was foul which made breathing difficult and, to top things off, the ubiquitous rats were constantly biting them as they worked.

When they had completed their tunnelling for the night they would cover over the entrance to the tunnel with a two-foot layer of straw. The guards never suspected a tunnel being dug right under their noses.

The officers' initial attempt came to an abrupt halt as they came across the foundations of the building. With the tools available to them, there was no way they could continue. They had to dig another tunnel, taking a different route and direction.

After tunnelling for a further twenty days they believed they had reached the desired exit point. They were wrong: the exit was directly next to a sentry box. They quickly covered it over and luckily were not detected.

The third and final attempt was successful. After thirty-eight days of digging, the men broke through to the surface, coming out in a storage shed of Kerr's Warehouse.

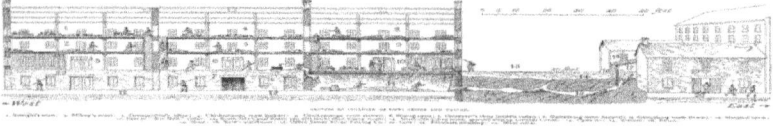

Colonel Thomas E. Rose, the escape leader, surveyed the location of the tunnel exit, and proclaimed to his diggers: 'The Underground Railroad to God's country is open!' Sometime after sundown on the night of February 9, 1864, Union officers began emerging from the tunnel in groups of two or three. They then began casually strolling through the front gate of the warehouse and headed north.

In all, one hundred and nine Federal officers emerged from the tunnel. It was not until late in the day of February 10 that repeated roll calls failed to account for the missing men. Frantic messages went out to local Confederate forces to apprehend the escapees. Nonetheless, over twelve hours passed before any Rebel response occurred.

Aftermath

Once the Confederates were made aware of the escape, search parties managed to recapture forty-eight of the prisoners, returning them to the prison. Two men tried to swim the James River and drowned. That left fifty-nine Union officers who escaped back to Union lines. The event was a tremendous morale boost for the Union Army.

Winston Churchill

Chapter 2

In 1895, Winston Churchill, a 2nd Lieutenant, 4th Queen's Own Hussars, began to take an interest in war correspondence in an effort to supplement the income he was receiving from his regiment. It was never his intention nor ambition to follow a conventional Army career but rather to seek out all possible chances of military action, using his mother's and family's influence in high society to arrange postings to active campaigns. He became a war correspondent for several London newspapers and wrote books about the campaigns.

On the 11 October 1899, the Second Boer War between Britain and the Boer Republics broke out. Churchill obtained a commission to act as war correspondent for *The Morning Post* with a salary of £250 per month. He accepted an invitation to accompany the 17th Lancers known as "Death or Glory Lads" on a raid against the Boers at Elandslaagte.

Winston and the Lancers were travelling on an armoured train, performing a reconnoitre between Frere and Chieveley in the British Natal Colony in November 1899. A Boer commando force had placed a big boulder on the track; the train rounded a bend, smashing into it. The locomotive derailed and the Boers opened up with field guns and rifle fire from various positions.

Those British soldiers who were uninjured returned fire, whilst others on the train did their best to get the injured and wounded out of harm's way. Although the carriages had derailed, the locomotive remained on the track. The soldiers attempted to uncouple the train, hoping to reverse back down the track however the incessant fire from the Boers made this a difficult task. Eventually the Boers swept down the hillside and captured the train and its occupants; a number of men were taken prisoner. Eventually the locomotive with some of the men escaped. Churchill found himself alone in a gully near the track. It was summer and the heat was stifling; he was covered in sweat, oil and dirt and was exhausted. A Boer officer dismounted from his horse, got down on one knee and raised his Mauser rifle. Churchill reached for the pistol and found his holster empty: he'd lost it on the train. He was defenceless and had no choice but to surrender.

The Boer officer took the young Winston into custody but what neither of them realised at the time was their destinies would cross again. Both these men would become prime ministers of their respective countries! Ironically their countries would fight in another war as allies in a few short years The Boer commander was General Louis Botha.

General Louis Botha

Churchill was a nondescript twenty- five year old at the time but was a member of an elite British family. His father, Lord Randolph Churchill, had been an eminent politician and the family bloodline went back to beyond the First Duke of Marlborough. The Boers knew they had a valuable prisoner who could be used in future negotiations with the British. The Boers, for many reasons, decided to treat Winston as a POW, despite the fact he was a civilian.

Winston Standing on the Right of Other British Prisoners

The prisoners were marched for some miles in the scorching heat before being loaded on a train heading for Pretoria. Along the way, they passed an imposing mountain, a mountain the British would rather forget, "Majuba Hill" came into view. Winston, however, remembered the mountain well it was here in February 1881, the Boers defeated the British army using their hit- and- run guerrilla warfare tactics. Soon after that humiliating defeat, the British negotiated a ceasefire thus ending the first Anglo-Boer War. This act of obtaining a ceasefire was described by the young Churchill as 'a disgraceful, cowardly peace.' After the Battle of Majuba, the British army never again wore their famous red tunics into battle; they adopted khaki combat uniforms thereafter.

Majuba Hill

British in Khaki

When the train transporting the prisoners passed by Majuba it was early evening and the light was fading. Churchill described the sight as 'a great dark mountain with memories as sad and gloomy as its appearance'.

The prisoners' train then continued on its journey to Pretoria

'I rode on home from Volksrust across the monotonous veld. Eventually the oh-so-familiar sight of Johannesburg's skyline about 15 miles away came into view, silhouetted against the late afternoon sun, signalling the end of another trip.'

Churchill and his colleagues were imprisoned in a converted school in the middle of Pretoria.

The prisoners were marched through the streets of Pretoria, reaching the prison school in the late afternoon. Churchill's observations on first sight of the State Model Schools building were:

'We turned a corner; on the other side of the road stood a long, low, red brick building with a slated veranda and a row of iron railings before it.'

Churchill decided quickly that captivity was not for him, thus he began to plot his escape on the first night at the prison school. On the night

of December 12th, when several prison guards had turned their backs, he took the opportunity to climb over the prison wall. Wearing a brown flannel suit with £75 in his pocket and four slabs of chocolate, Churchill walked leisurely on through the night, in the hope of finding the Delagoa Bay Railway. So began his great escape and journey to freedom.

Churchill jumped onto a train and hid among soft sacks covered in coal dust. Leaving the train before daybreak, he continued on his escape. Lady luck was on his side, when Winston happened upon the home of Mr John Howard, manager of the Transvaal Collieries. He knocked on the front door; Mr Howard's response to his plea for help was 'Thank God you have come here! It is the only house for twenty miles where you would not have been handed over. We are all British here, we will see you through.'

Mr Howard first hid Churchill in a coalmine, which made the young Winston quite ill, after which, Mr Howard transported him to safety. Churchill had to squeeze into a hole at the end of a train car loaded with bales of wool. This was a very uncomfortable journey.

Once he arrived in Durban, a British stronghold, he was hailed as a hero.

Captain William Leefe Robinson

Zeppelin

Chapter 3

William Leefe Robinson was the youngest of seven children, born in Southern India on the 14th July 1895. His father, Horace Robinson, had a coffee plantation and the family was quite wealthy.

Young William or Billy as he was called had a privileged childhood and as the youngest child tended to be spoiled not only by his parents but his older sisters.

Life was one big playground and for the cheeky Billy, education was a very firm last on his list of priorities.

He attended "Dragon School" at Oxford for a year before returning to India to complete his education in Bangalore at the "Bishop Cotton School". Billy then went on to secondary education at "St Bees College" Cumbria. Unlike his elder brother who excelled in school Billy barley passed his grades.

It was sport where William excelled; he won his house cap for football, was a key member of the hockey team and was a keen rower.

Billy enjoyed the London social scene with trips to the theatre and many parties to attend. The dashing young man was also very popular with the young ladies. A promotion to Sergeant in the school's Officer Training Corp was seen as a very positive move by his parents.

Things were about to change for William and the entire family as 1914 approached, two of his sisters married and he was appointed head of Eaglesfield House. He also enjoyed his time with the OTC and experienced life in the army at various camps.

In March 1915 he joined the Royal Flying Corps, and was posted to No 4 Squadron at St Omer. His role was to fly a BE2cs on reconnaissance patrols over German lines. It was during one of these flights he received shrapnel wounds and was on sick leave for a month.

Reporting back for duty at Farnborough on 29th June 1915 he began flying immediately.

On 2nd February 1916, Robinson was transferred to Sutton's Farm at Hornchurch. Part of 19th Reserve Squadron under Major T. C. Higgins. This airfield was nothing more than a paddock, which they shared with sheep, which often invaded the runway. The hangers were merely tents housing two aircraft. The squadron soon grew to eighteen aircraft and wooden hangers replaced the tents.

On the afternoon of the 2nd September 1916, sixteen airships, twelve from the German Naval Airship Division and four from the Army Division, set out for England on what was to be the biggest air raid of the war. The Zeppelins were carrying thirty-two tons of bombs. The Germans were going to teach the English a lesson they would never forget.

Zeppelin Over England

In command of the lead airship was Hauptmann Wilhelm Schramm, an experienced captain who knew the London area well. He was born at Old Charlton, Kent, and lived in England until the age of fifteen. Each Zeppelin had a crew of sixteen comprising of machinists, gunners, an 'elevator' man and 'bomb' man, officers and Captain.

At approximately 11pm the Home Defence squadrons were put on alert. Radio messages from the airships had been intercepted, and a welcoming party was prepared. Ten aircraft were sent up that night. First away was William Robinson, the fog was thick but Robinson was convinced it would be clear at a higher altitude. He had three drums of ammunition and just enough fuel to keep him aloft for three and a half hours.

The Zeppelins approached London from the north passing over Royston and Hitchin dropping their bombs over what they believed to be the London docks. Lehmann, an experienced captain, took his ship up to 13,000 feet. One of the crew spotted an aircraft approaching the airship. Robinson had seen the Zeppelin illuminated by searchlights and had climbed up to meet it. Lehmann, with a much lighter ship now that half his bombs were gone, promptly headed for cloud and continued to climb. He disappeared. Robinson was concerned he had already been in the air for two hours and had only one and a half hours flying time left.

Half an hour later, Lehmann was wreaking destruction over North London. The Finsbury and Victoria Park searchlights found him over Alexandra Palace the gunners filled the sky with anti aircraft fire. The zeppelin captain turned his craft and headed for Walthamstow trying to dodge the searchlights. Hundreds of Londoners watched, but no matter how close they burst, the ground defence's shells seemed to have no effect.

Robinson had given up searching for the airship he had lost in the clouds, attracted by the activity over Ponder's End he headed for what he presumed must be another airship. William spotted the airship being blasted by shellfire and headed straight for the Zeppelin. The watching crowd below swelled as the news spread that a pilot was within striking distance of the hated 'Zepp'. Then, the firing stopped, the searchlights swung frantically searching for the enemy, the airship found cloud cover and disappeared from sight.

As suddenly as it had vanished, the airship reappeared. Every gun roared and the night sky came alive again. Robinson's aircraft was rocked by the blasts, but closed in.

His first drum of ammunition was ready; he flew alongside the airship firing his guns riddling the fuselage with bullets. Turning his aeroplane around he viewed the Zeppelin. The airship appeared to be completely unharmed by the attack. Robinson raked the length of the vessel a second time. Still, there was no real damage. It seemed the massive craft was impregnable. William had one drum of ammunition left and very little fuel. The plane was now behind and slightly below the airship, he decided to change tactics. He dived at the thin end of the craft, heading for the twin rudders above and below the elevators. He fired into that one area. Now the guns of the ground defences were silent and all eyes were fixed on the airship. They had no idea what the pilot was doing. Within seconds the tail section was alight, and flames over one hundred feet burst out into the darkness. It did not take long for the entire Zeppelin to be in flames. The hydrogen that kept it

31

airborne ignited turning night into day. The spectators were enthralled.

The blazing wreckage of the Zeppelin slowly fell to earth.

William Robinson turned his plane for home feeling an incredible sense of achievement.

Airship Wreck

With his fuel tanks almost empty he landed at Sutton's Farm at 2.45am three and a half hours after take-off, he was exhausted. The excited ground crews milled around the aircraft, with a cheer they lifted the hero shoulder high in triumph from his aircraft to the office.

The Zeppelin Crew Burial

"I recommend Lieut W. L. Robinson for the Victoria Cross for the most conspicuous gallantry displayed in this successful attack."

Lieutenant General Henderson

The V.C. was awarded.

On the 5th September 1916, the London Gazette announced the award;

"War Office 5th September 1916. His Majesty the King has been graciously pleased to award the Victoria Cross to the undermentioned officer, Lieutenant William Leefe Robinson, Worcestershire Regiment and Royal Flying Corps. For most conspicuous bravery. He attacked an enemy airship under circumstances of great difficulty

33

and danger, and sent it crashing to the ground as a flaming wreck. He had been in the air for more than two hours and had previously attacked another airship during his flight."

The British public had discovered the perfect 'gentleman' hero.

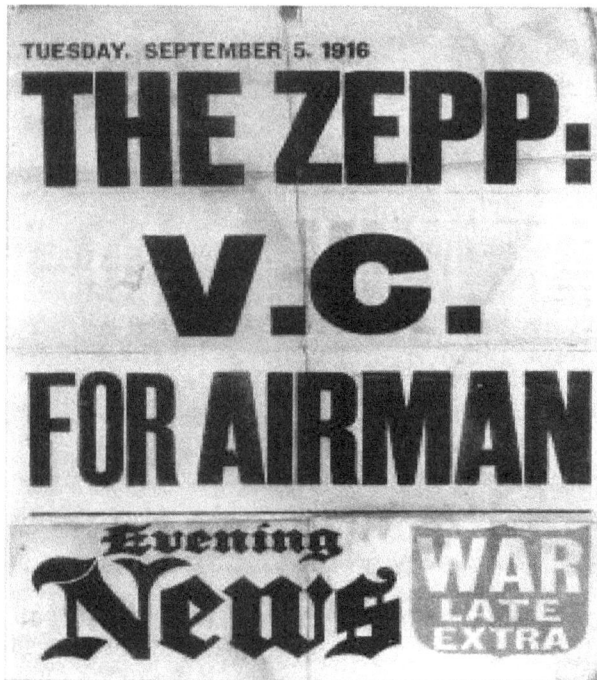

TUESDAY, SEPTEMBER 5. 1916
THE ZEPP:
V.C.
FOR AIRMAN
Evening News
WAR LATE EXTRA

RUMANIA EXPOSES GERMAN STORY OF "DEFEAT."

DAILY SKETCH.

GUARANTEED DAILY NETT SALE MORE THAN 1,000,000 COPIES.

No. 2,543.   LONDON, SATURDAY, SEPTEMBER 9, 1916.   [Registered as a Newspaper.]   ONE HALFPENNY.

AIRMAN V.C. AT WINDSOR CASTLE.

The young V.C. himself in the streets of Windsor yesterday.

The modest hero's arrival.

The crowd and many others dismissed by the belief that the V.C. was not coming.

Lieutenant Robinson leaving the Castle.

Lieutenant W. Leefe Robinson, the young airman who brought down the Zeppelin, received his V.C. from the King at Windsor Castle yesterday. A large crowd, including the Mayoress and many notabilities, which assembled to welcome him at the railway station, waited awhile, and then dispersed disappointed. The faithfulness of his escort had delayed the V.C.'s arrival. Lieutenant Robinson, however, was not too late to receive his decoration from the King, and afterwards he had a great reception from his admirers in the streets.—(Daily Sketch Photographs.)

Don't Mess With The Red Baron

Chapter 4

Robinson was not to fly again for the next three months he was obligated to the air force to attend many official engagements. He was England's hero but this was not to Robinson's liking, he was an airman; he wanted to fly!

Eventually he was promoted to Flight Commander and temporary Captain but he still did not have a posting, this created much anxiety. He was offered a command with the Home Defence Squadron in Northern England and Scotland but this was not why he enlisted. He decided to volunteer for duty in France.

Finally on 9th February 1917 a posting came through. Robinson joined 48 Squadron at Rendcombe in Gloucester, under Major L. Parker. The squadron was eagerly awaiting the arrival of new aircraft prior to their posting to France. Robinson's wish had been granted, but he would not have long to enjoy his new position.

Bristol F2a

Equipped with eighteen Bristol F2a's, 48 Squadron flew to France on 18th March 1917. The aeroplanes were to prove excellent fighters in the years to come, but in the early weeks there were problems. The new Constantinesco Synchronising gear for the forward firing Vickers gun proved to be unreliable. A more severe problem was the Vickers and Lewis guns jammed at high altitude. It was thought that the lubricating oil was freezing; Robinson suggested the guns be used without oil.

The first flight of new Bristols took off from La Bellevue airfield on 5th April. Robinson was in command with Lieutenant Edward Warburton as observer. He led his patrol in a tight formation believing the protection this provided was extremely important.

The Bristol had not yet been fully appreciated as an offensive weapon and Robinson and his squadron were not totally conversant with the fighting tactics being employed by the Germans over the Western Front.

He was therefore, totally unprepared for a clash with Germany's most famous and successful flying ace.

Rittmeister Manfred Frhr. von ... en

Freiherr von Richthofen "The Red Baron"

Leutnant Manfred Freiherr von Richthofen ("Red Baron") was leading a squadron of five twin-gun Albatros D111 fighters, spotting the six Bristols they attacked The Germans scattered the British twin seaters and within minutes four had been forced down behind enemy lines. Vizefeldwebel Sebastian Festner brought Robinson down near Mericourt both he and Warburton were immediately captured. They were held for a few days in Karlsruhe, and then transferred to the prisoner-of-war camp in Freiberg-in-Breisgau.

The loss of four Bristol fighters came as a blow to the hard-pressed Royal Flying Corps now fighting a desperate and losing battle against a superior enemy. However, the loss of Robinson himself was a devastating blow. There were reports he had been killed and the news stunned the nation. A letter written to his beloved Joan confirming he was a prisoner brought much relief to the many people who had taken this British hero to heart.

Can't Help Myself

Just Have to Escape

Chapter 5

For Robinson the next twenty months proved to be difficult. He was as famous in Germany as he was in England, but in Germany he wasn't adored he was loathed.

The German prison authorities and the guards who were charged with his detention mistreated badly.

The reason for this treatment was not only because he had been awarded a V.C. and revered as a hero, it was because he was a habitual "escaper".

Soon after arriving in Freiburg Robinson and his good friend Second Lieutenant Baerlin of 16 Squadron attempted to dig a tunnel under the perimeter fence but were apprehended by guards.

The second attempt was made with the aid of a guard who they attempted to bribe; despite the guard accepting the offer the attempt failed. The authorities heard of the plot and Robinson and Baerlin were arrested; a date was set for a formal court martial.

With incredible bravado, Robinson promptly attempted to escape again A gate to a courtyard had remained unlocked deliberately; he and his cohorts opened it and hung their washing on the line. This was meant to conceal the movements of the escapers. A locked door stood between the prisoners and freedom. The plan included an orderly who had been a locksmith prior to the war. He role was to pick the lock. However, he refused at the last minute in case he was caught by the guards and punished severely for aiding an escape.

The third plan had failed; the inner door was shut once again, and the Germans knew nothing of the attempt.

A fourth plan was formed within twenty-four hours of the third plan being abandoned. A tunnel was dug under their barracks a staircase was uncovered which led to an adjoining church. The group of officers forming the escape party gathered in the church. Prising open a window the first man climbed through and dropped into the street below. The streets of Freiburg had become familiar to the prisoners during their daytime excursions. They quickly made their way out of town and split up. Robinson, Baerlin and another officer made their way towards the Swiss frontier. Travelling at night, they eventually arrived at the border. Four miles outside Stohlingen, and four miles from freedom, all three were arrested.

After four attempts in as many months, Robinson's reputation as a troublemaker had well and truly been established. In October the court martial commenced, he was sentenced to a months' solitary confinement. Baerlin was sentenced to three months. They were sent to the underground fortress of Zorndorf; a daunting place.

There had never been an escape from Zorndorf. Underground tunnels led to the dark cells. The only exit was up a long sloping tunnel, which emerged in the centre of a mound, ringed by wire and searchlights. Robinson said very little about his time as a prisoner at Zorndorf when he returned to England. Without doubt this must have been the worst of his experiences. To a man who suffered from claustrophobia solitary confinement underground must have been a living nightmare.

On the 2nd May 1918 Robinson was transferred to a third camp Clausthal, in the Hartz Mountains. Along with two other officers he was boarded onto a train. Immediately an escape plan was hatched. One officer was to distract one of the guards while the other two made a jump for it. The plan was fraught with danger and unfortunately for Robinson, he didn't make it.

Clausthal Prison

Arriving at Clausthal, Robinson was met by one the infamous Niemeyer twins, Heinrich. Heinrich and Karl Niemeyer were Commandants of Clausthal and Holzminden camps respectively. Their harsh treatment of prisoners was legendary. They had spent some time in America before the war and had learnt a little rudimentary English including many swear words. Their fits of rage directed at the prisoners uttering stupid threats in very strange English would have been hilarious if it had been in other circumstances. In the POW camps where the Commandants had wide ranging powers, the brothers were feared and hated not just by the prisoners, but by the German guards also.

Heinrich Niemeyer, nick named by the prisoners as "Milwaukee Bill," took an instant dislike to Robinson whose reputation had preceded him. Initially, life was tolerable. Robinson received the privileges due to an officer P.O.W. and his pass card survives; evidence that he was allowed a certain amount of freedom. In view of his preoccupation with escaping, the wording of the card is a little ironic.

"By this card I give my word of honour that during the walks outside the camp, I will not escape nor attempt to make an escape, nor will I make any preparations to do so, nor will I attempt to commit any action during this time to the prejudice of the German Empire. I give hereby my word of honour to use this card only myself and not give it to any other prisoner of war."

The Red Cross was active at Clausthal; their mandate was to ensure life was as comfortable as possible for all prisoners. Letters from home helped to keep morale reasonably high. Robinson's mail included letters from well wishers who still remembered the "Hero of Cuffley."

Robinson's time at Clausthal came to an end in July 1918.

In his book "Cage Birds" Squadron leader H. E. Hervey M.C. who knew Robinson well and shared in many of the attempted escapes, remembers his departure.

> *"This month Robinson left the camp. The Commandant had taken an instant dislike to him at their first meeting, probably as a result of Robinson's reputation. Anyway, he seized the first opportunity of getting rid of him, and handed him over to the tender care of his brother at Holzminden. Robinson was a cheerful soul and I regretted his departure, for, since our first encounter at Douai the day after I was shot down, we had moved together from camp to camp. I never saw him again."*

Holzminden

Karl Niemeyer Commandant

The last camp to hold William Leefe Robinson was Holzminden. Here, under Karl Niemeyer, William was treated cruelly and was continually persecuted. Robinson didn't help things much when at the first opportunity he escaped with another officer, Captain W. S. Stephenson of 73 Squadron. Karl Niemeyer detested escapers; he saw them as deliberately undermining his position and credibility with his superior officers. They were both recaptured and Robinson was thrown into solitary confinement. Niemeyer raged and shouted at him using his crazy American-English.

H. G. Durnford of the R.A.F. was British Adjutant at Holzminden. In his book "The "Tunnellers of Holzminden" he describes the treatment meted out to officers who attempted to escape.

'They were locked in the ground floor cells of "A" Kaserne where the "flies and staleness of the atmosphere were correspondingly oppressive . . . These particular rooms used to be visited two or three times a night by a Feldwebel with an electric torch, which he used to flash on the occupant of each bed in turn, thereby effectively waking everybody up.'

Robinson was about to embark on his greatest escape not alone but with more than fifty of his fellow officers. He had to conquer his greatest fear, claustrophobia, if he was to be successful in his final escape.

The Blonde Devil

Chapter 6

The little blonde boy was running amongst the street traders and food stalls with his elder brother Hans, laughing as they played hide and seek with their friends. Living in Rome had its benefits including playing amongst the ruins of ancient Rome and pretending to be soldiers or gladiators conquering all before them.

The boys would always be on the lookout for ancient artefacts, which could be sold to the tourists at much-inflated prices. The neighbours nicknamed him 'the blonde devil' but his real name was Gunther and apart from his German name he would be taken as an Italian boy from the north.

Gunther's parents, Edouard and Hermione were of good stock, his father was the son of the illegitimate son of Duke Friedrich Ludwig, his mother was the daughter of a well know cigar manufacturer. Painters, writers, artists and musicians constantly graced the Plüschow's dinner table. The house was always filled with intelligent conversation and laughter, all encouraged by copious amounts of wine and grappa.

Gunther and Hans were hiding under the table while a serious conversation was taking place about Germany's ambitions in Europe.

'I don't understand any of what they are all talking about,' whispered Hans to his young brother.

'Me neither, but we should be able to steal a bottle while they are all talking.'

Gunther reached up from under the table and felt around blindly for a bottle of wine. Someone grabbed his hand and he looked up to see a man with a black beard and long hair. The man grinned and passed a half bottle down to him, which he shared with his brother under the olive tree in the back courtyard.

'Hans, I feel a little dizzy.'

'Me too.'

The two boys crept up to their bedroom and lay down on their beds and went to sleep immediately.

Gunther woke up with the vile smell of vomit surrounding him in the bed. He had thrown up in his sleep.

He quickly got up and washed himself and stripped the bed. It was when he attempted to wash the sheets that his mother caught him.

'Not really worth it was it son?

'No mother.'

Another lesson learned!

Gunther's parents decided now was the time to enrol him in a French Jesuit school where he excelled, especially in languages.

Unfortunately Edouard, Gunther's father fell ill and they decided to move the family back to Germany to settle in his mother's hometown of Bünde, a small picturesque village on the River Else.

Gunther loved his new surroundings and made many new friends; his best friend was a sixty-year-old sailor, Karl, who taught the ten-year-old boy how to sail; they could be seen skimming across the lake all afternoon in a small yacht.

A life changing event 1896 he followed in his brother's footsteps and joined the cadet institute at Plön.

Gunther's military career had begun.

He arrived at cadet school on a beautiful summer's day and observed the magnificent lake with a chain of smaller lakes surrounding the town. He approached the stately seventeenth century manor house that was to be his home for the next few years. For a boy of ten used to getting his own way, it was going to be a significant learning experience.

Gunther and his Father at the Academy

An officer approached the new recruits and addressed them in a very stern tone.

'You are all entering cadet school as little boys; you will eventually graduate as officers of the great German army. Between now and graduation you will learn discipline, sailing, military history and many other military subjects. You are to form a queue in front of the medical office and be examined; we don't want any sickly lads joining this academy.'

They all lined up and were called in one by one, Gunther passed with flying colours.

The next examination was academic. If the recruits failed they were excused from the academy and their dejected parents were asked to take them home. Gunther was a very intelligent boy and marked as one of the brightest in the current intake.

The new recruits then ate a meal together in the grand dinning hall and got the chance to meet some of the other young cadets.

Gunther enjoyed the occasions when he could wear his dress uniform with red shoulder straps and cuff facings but the majority of the time he and the other cadets were required to wear a very drab uniform of grey and black. Being located on the lakes meant plenty of opportunity to pilot small, military craft and other boats of all sorts and sizes. Karl, the old sailor had taught him well and he excelled as he did in swimming and rowing.

Academically Gunther also did very well with military history being his favourite subject.

The turn of the century would bring great changes to the world including Gunther's, he turned fourteen in 1900 and said good-bye to Plön and commenced the next stage of his military education. He entered the Imperial Military Academy at Gross-Lichterfield close to Berlin.

As before in the junior academy they all ate their first meal in the grand dinning room. An officer gave the welcoming speech.

'You have chosen the finest profession that there is on earth. You have the highest goal in sight... We teach you here to fulfil this goal. You are here about to learn what confers significance first to last in your life. You are here to learn about death. From now on you no longer have free will; you will have to learn to obey, later to be able to command...

Gunther went to bed with these words ringing in his ears.

Gunther and his classmates suffered the normal abuse from the older boys as part of their initiation. It wasn't too bad as it was thought they had already suffered enough at the junior academy; they were right.

Gunther gathered some like-minded cadets and formed a "navigators club" they would frequent the academy library and dream of trips to far away lands with exotic sounding names. On one such day he was taken with Tierra del Fuego at the bottom of South America, icy mountains, glaciers, beautiful forests and fast rivers. He tore the pages from the book and told the other club members 'this is mine, only I go there.'

Years later Gunther did go and there's a memorial to him and his exploration feats.

Free as a Bird

Chapter 7

China 1914

The young German aviator, Gunther Plüschow was flying over the green hills of northern China looking out for Japanese planes. He knew they were superior in both speed and manoeuvrability.

He was the sole airman located in the German colony of Tsingtau (now Qingdao) in China. His role was to provide a reconnaissance capability to the German fleet stationed there. Repeatedly flying his aircraft singled handed, he was constantly outnumbered by the Japanese "Farman" Float Planes, but he persevered, spotting artillery and troop movements well over enemy lines.

It was a particularly sunny clear day and although he had not seen any enemy movements he was in very good spirits. Being stationed at Tsingtao was to his liking. The weather was good: mild winters and warm summers, the British and German girls were pretty and there was an endless supply of good German beer.

Coming into land his mood changed.

The Taube's engine had cut out and would not re-start.

Looking down to his right he saw the Polo Club and a bloody deep ditch; on his left was the hotel: his only option was to go straight ahead and crash into a small wood.

'OK, here goes, I need to try and get some more altitude.'

The altitude lever failed. The Taube began skimming over the tree-tops and came to a stop in a large ditch. She certainly didn't look the graceful dove to which "Taube" translated; her nose was down, her tail in the air.

Gunther climbed out of the cockpit and assessed the situation.

'Well, it could have been worse; I could be dead!'

Looking at the crash site made him realise he'd missed the cable between two telegraph poles by the closest of margins. He could have been decapitated!

Gunther tried to assess the damage to the Taube; the engine was in one piece and the wings could be mended. The wires could be untangled and the canvas could be stitched. The propeller however, was a write off.

'Thank God we have spare parts back in the hangar,' he thought.

By this time, his mechanic, Franz Stuben had arrived on the scene and was inspecting the damage.

'Well, Gunther, you certainly messed up our beautiful bird didn't you?'

'The bloody engine cut out, Franz! You're the one that's supposed to keep it going!'

'OK, OK, let's get back to the hangar and open the crates; we should have all the parts we need. It should be fine, just a lot of hard work and we'll get you up there again.'

The two men walked back the three kilometres to the hangar and started to pry open the crates.

'Fucking hell! What's that smell?' exclaimed Franz

'It smells like a dead rat' said Gunther.

When the top of the crate had been pried open they were greeted with the sight of the wing ribs and other timber parts covered in a fungus. The canvas covers were also completely rotten.

'Take a look at the propellers, Franz six spare and all useless. What in the hell are we going to do now?'

'We're going to rebuild your aeroplane; don't worry about the propeller I'll think of something.'

With the help of two sailors and eight Chinese labourers recruited from the dockyard, they rebuilt the aircraft minus its propeller in a week.

Franz knew the Chinese were fantastic at copying. They had a reputation to reproduce anything.

'Let's take the best propeller as our model and make a pattern. One of the Chinese reckoned the carpenter on the outskirts of the village, Tao Li, would be able to make us a new one.'

The two Germans and four Chinese workers carried the propeller up to Tao's workshop. Seven sections were shaped from oak planks and glued together with carpenter's glue. Not perfect but it would do the job.

When the glue had set they lugged it back down to the hangar and attached to the bedraggled bird.

Gunther stood back and gazed at this patched- up ugly duckling and wondered how in the hell he would take off from the tiny airfield. Franz, Gunther and the two sailors wheeled her out onto the runway.

'Gunther, you have to be confident she will fly again. It's no use getting in the cockpit again if you don't believe in her and your own ability.' Said Franz.

'I'm confident that I'll be shitting myself, Franz, but I'll give it my best shot.'

Gunther climbed up into the cockpit, checked the instruments and made sure the altitude lever and control stick worked. He gave the lads the thumbs up and they turned the makeshift propeller. After a few false starts, the engine burst into life sounding reasonably normal.

He revved the engines and released the brakes as Franz and one of the sailors removed the wheel chocks. The Taube started down the runway gathering speed and eventually lifted off.

Gunther soon realised that the plane was slower with the replacement propeller but nevertheless, she would do the job. After a thirty-minute flight, he landed safely and taxied over to the hangar where Franz and the others were waiting. An inspection of the propeller revealed the layers of oak were starting to come apart.

'I'm glad the prop didn't separate whilst I was at three thousand feet!'

They solved the problem by gluing it back together and that's what Gunther did after each flight. After the first few flights he added canvas and plaster to the edge of the blades to hold the whole thing together. It was a precarious way to stay airborne!

The relationship between Britain and Germany had deteriorated by August 1914. The Japanese had jumped at the chance to join Britain in the war against Germany in Asia. Britain immediately regretted giving them the invitation. Britain could see that Japan would take over the territory formally occupied by the Germans and not return it to the rightful owners, China.

Japan gave Germany an ultimatum to leave China and decommission its war ships.

Germany refused. The war was about to engulf Tsingtao and the surrounding territory.

It was a fine Sunday morning; Gunther was flying low over enemy territory when he spotted a Japanese column just sixty miles from Tsingtao. No sooner had he spotted them than they started shooting at him with rifle and machinegun. He was unarmed so he made a quick retreat and landed safely. On examining the plane, he found ten bullet holes through the Taube's fuselage. His solution to the problem was to not fly so low in the future.

Tsingtao soon became blockaded and surrounded by Japanese and British forces. On November 5th the Japanese forces were, in some cases, only 100 meters from the German trenches. The constant shelling by the Japanese forces over the previous weeks had reduced these trenches to rubble pits, offering little or no protection from the enemy's gunfire. Gunther had to admire the accuracy of the Japanese artillery: after all, they had been trained by the German army in Berlin.

Plüschow was given orders by the Governor of Tsingtao, Meyer-Waldeck, to avoid capture and return to Germany carrying important papers back to German High Command.

He returned to the villa which he'd called home for the past twelve months and gathered some possessions he could take. The space limitations in the plane ensured it wasn't much.

He opened the stable door and let his horse "Fips" run free - in the opposite direction, he hoped, from the Japanese onslaught. He then let his chickens free; he would miss their magnificent eggs.

He strode down the pathway to the airstrip and examined the maps he was intending to use to make good his escape. Once he was sure of his route he visited a battery commanded by his good friend, Julius Aye. The view from the post reminded Gunther of Dante's Inferno, large guns flashing their fire, shells exploding all around and men dying. Julius too died the day after Gunther left for Mainland China.

Gunther's Taube, the World's first Fighter Plane

It was an icy cold morning in Tsingtao. The mist rolled over the ground and enveloped all in its path.

'I don't like your chances of getting airborne this morning, Gunther. You may have to wait for the fog to lift,' said his mechanic.

'I don't really have a choice. My orders are to leave this morning. It is imperative I deliver these papers to Bismarck in Berlin as soon as possible.'

'How far do you think you can get in the old girl?'

'Don't know, but when she runs out of fuel I'll find other ways to make it back.'

Gunther's dog, Husdent, sat at his feet waiting for a pat, little did he know that it would be the last caress from the master he adored.

Gunther Plüschow outside the walls of Tsingtao, China

Plüschow flew out of Tsingtao surrounded by heavy anti-aircraft fire from the surrounding hills that were swarming with Japanese soldiers. He flew as far as his 'Taube' would carry him, landing in Mainland China, a neutral country. His great adventure had just begun.

This Must be China

Chapter 8

Gunther's planned route was to fly to a village called Haichow about 200 kilometres from Tsingtao in Kiangsu province not far from the yellow sea. There he would refuel there and fly to Shanghai where he would meet up with some German friends.

His navigation tools comprised a compass and an old map and with these and some good luck, he arrived over Haichow in the early morning. Looking from both sides of the plane trying to find a suitable landing spot, which proved to be difficult there had been monsoon rains and all the paddocks were flooded. The only dry spots seemed to have houses or cemeteries on them and it was not his intention to visit the latter just yet!

At last he spotted a field he thought would be suitable: just as well, as his fuel gauge was showing empty. His experience of landing in tight airfields put him in good stead and he touched down without too much drama however the plane immediately sank into thick mud. The plane stopped suddenly with the Taube once again ending up with its nose down and its tail in the air. The makeshift propeller was completely destroyed.

It didn't take long for the field to fill with Chinese villagers all in awe of this huge bird that had flown in and landed next to their village.

Gunther waved but got no reaction; he then dug into his pockets and threw out some coins, a gesture which worked a treat.

'Excuse me, are you OK?'

Gunther couldn't believe his ears an American accent speaking English amongst the constant chattering of Chinese!

'Would you like a hand getting down from your plane?'

'Yes, thank you.'

The tall American climbed up onto the wing and helped Gunter from the cockpit.

'Welcome to Haichow. My name is Lorenzo - Dr Lorenzo Morgan.'

'Hello, Lorenzo. I am Gunther Plüschow.'

Gunther handed him the passport that Meyer-Waldeck had given him before his departure. Lorenzo called one of the villagers over and instructed him in fluent Mandarin to take Gunther's passport to the local chief mandarin.

It was always best to keep the most powerful man in the village happy.

Lorenzo invited Gunther back to his home where he met his wife, also a doctor.

A squad of Chinese soldiers arrived and surrounded the plane, protecting her from damage or looting.

The Americans made Gunther very welcome serving him a delicious breakfast. A Chinese officer called at the Morgan home to

63

inform them that a guard of honour had surrounded the house and the local mandarin would be arriving shortly to meet their esteemed guest.

Gunther asked the Morgans if he could borrow some tools to dismantle the plane but the only tools he found in their shed was an axe and an antique saw.

Try as he might, he didn't get far, so he gave in to the inevitable and torched his beloved Taube.

That evening the mandarin's personal 'litter' arrived to accompany him back to enjoy a feast fit for a king. Eight burly men carried him for the forty-minutes journey. Chinese soldiers with their bayonets fixed and a band of musicians making a horrendous noise also accompanied him!

Once he arrived there were more musicians, more soldiers and a bevy of local dignitaries very keen to meet him.

The banquet began with Gunther seated next to the mandarin and some of his wives. After the thirty- sixth course, Gunther was feeling rather full.

Later in the evening, with Lorenzo acting as interpreter, he answered everybody's questions.

The next morning Gunther embarked on the next stage of his journey to Nanking and then on to Shanghai. He then boarded a junk and set sail on a very uncomfortable cold journey. It took five days to reach Nanking. An English language newspaper, "The Shanghai Times" was given to him. There was a deep disappointment upon reading an account of how Tsingtao had fallen to the Japanese and how they defeated an ill-disciplined drunken German garrison. He knew the opposite was true but the newspaper was partly owned by the Japanese.

A German torpedo captain met Plüschow on his arrival. It was good to speak to a fellow countryman. His name was Helmut Brunner and he accompanied Gunther to his quarters where he and his crew were staying as the guests of the Chinese Government.

Brunner showed Gunther his quarters. Gunther protested to the German that he was merely stopping over on his way to Shanghai and he would not be staying in Nanking long. The pilot insisted on meeting the governor but he was not available, so a Government official met with him and wished him a happy and comfortable stay in Nanking. Gunther left the building and as soon as he climbed into his carriage, a Chinese soldier stepped in as well. It was explained to him that this soldier was his guard of honour.

Losing the guard and getting to the railway station that night was imperative. A formal dinner was being held at the home of a German resident that night and Gunther along with some other German officers had been invited. Towards the end of the evening, a houseboy was sent out to tell his guard of honour that Gunther had already left thirty minutes prior along with some other German officers. All German officers looked pretty much the same to a Chinese foot soldier so he started to run down the road to try and catch up.

A carriage was brought around the back of the residence and it took Gunther to the train station where he purchased a ticket; the guard took no notice of him as he passed through the gate.

The trip went without incident and on arrival in the early morning he simply walked past the guard and hailed a rickshaw to take him to a German friend's home where for the first time since he left Tsingtao, he felt he could relax.

For the next three weeks Gunther enjoyed meeting some of his countrymen including Otto who was also at Tsingtao when he was stationed there. Otto escaped the Japanese by impersonating a Chinese worker; he simply walked out of the town and through various means, ended up in Shanghai.

Gunther did not trust anybody with his travel plans so he spread the word that he was going to catch a train to Peking (Beijing) and present himself to the German embassy.

He'd been given a new identity, Mr E. F. McGarvin, a sales representative for the Singer Sewing Machine Company.

A friend of Plüschow's arranged for him to be taken by boat to an industrial area upstream where he was to stay for a few days in a dingy, tiny little room in an apartment block. There were some British people staying in the same block so Gunther feigned madness so they would leave him alone. He quite enjoyed being mad for that short time.

America

Chapter 9

Finally it was time to board the SS Mongolia, which was due to sail for San Francisco on15th December 1914. He had one problem: he had only one piece of luggage, this was very unusual for such a voyage. He knew that an observant crewmember might question his lack of baggage.

He quizzed his cabin steward why he hadn't received his other two bags loaded the day before. He made such a fuss that he had the stewards running around trying to find the fictitious luggage but to no avail.

The SS Mongolia steamed out of Shanghai harbour on a beautiful calm morning. Gunther knew that there were more perils ahead; they were heading for Japan. They were due to dock at three Japanese ports. He devised a plan after meeting the ship's doctor, an American. He took the risk of divulging to the doctor who he was whereupon the doctor showed great empathy and agreed to help Plüschow. The doctor suggested he feign sickness and therefore could not leave his cabin. The ship birthed at Nagasaki three days later and Japanese officials boarded and assembled all the passengers in the grand saloon to conduct a roll call and check documents. When Plüschow's name was called, the ship's doctor stepped forward and explained that the missing passenger had a high fever and he believed Plüschow was suffering from a highly contagious disease. The officials were unconvinced and demanded to see the sick passenger. Gunther did a fantastic job writhing and moaning under the bed covers. The officials did not want to enter the cabin and cleared Gunther without actually seeing him.

The SS Mongolia went on to berth at Kobe and Yokohama and in each port the same superb acting took place with the same result.

On board was a journalist named Brace who would often be seen with Gunther once they left Japanese waters. They talked about Gunther's experiences at Tsingtao and his flight to China and the subsequent adventures. What Gunther didn't realise was that Brace was composing a story which he intended to send back to his newspaper in the USA. By the time the SS Mongolia birthed in Honolulu, it was spread across the local papers. Gunther had to keep reminding himself that the USA was neutral in the conflict and he had become a celebrity in America. One American passenger suggested he could earn a very good living by writing about his experiences.

On 29 December, 1914, the ship docked in San Francisco where he could now drop the false name and revert back to his real name; he was now in safe waters.

The quayside was teaming with reporters and photographers waiting for a glimpse of the daring German aviator who found it difficult to be polite with all of them pushing and shoving to extract a few words from him.

'I have nothing to say. I will be writing my own story.'

With that, he pushed his way through the crowd and hailed a taxi.

In March, 1915, his first article was published in *Sunset Magazine* , entitled "Flying Under Fire".

Gunther enjoyed his newfound freedom and became part of the social elite attending dinner parties and other social functions. The American Government took no interest whatsoever.

Gunther in San Francisco

However, he was still a member of the Imperial German Navy and his country was at war; he needed to return to Germany. On 2 January 1915, he boarded a train, which would take him to Chicago. The scenery, including the Grand Canyon, enthralled him. Upon reaching Chicago he disembarked and boarded another train to Virginia where he was due to meet an old friend. The friend advised him that the best way to get back to Germany was to travel to New York and board a ship for Europe. So the journey continued travelling by train to New York where he would meet some friends who would assist him in boarding an appropriate ship.

Arrangements would take a few weeks, which was disappointing.

It was during his stay that he discovered a strong anti-German sentiment amongst the American press. Headlines appeared, such as "Germans Said to Have Shot Many Priests": apparently Catholic clergy had been "beaten, tortured, and executed".

Plüschow was very disappointed that these reports were published and believed. He wrote: 'Hardly a picture, hardly a newspaper... did not incite hatred against Germany...'

Gunther's desire to get back to Germany was immense. An introduction to an expert forger enabled him to purchase a passport that would pass even the closest scrutiny. Subsequently, he became Ernst Suse, a Swiss locksmith.

Boarding the "Duca degli Abruzzi" on 30 January, 1915, as a third class passenger entitled him to be housed in the steerage. This was not going to be a comfortable voyage!

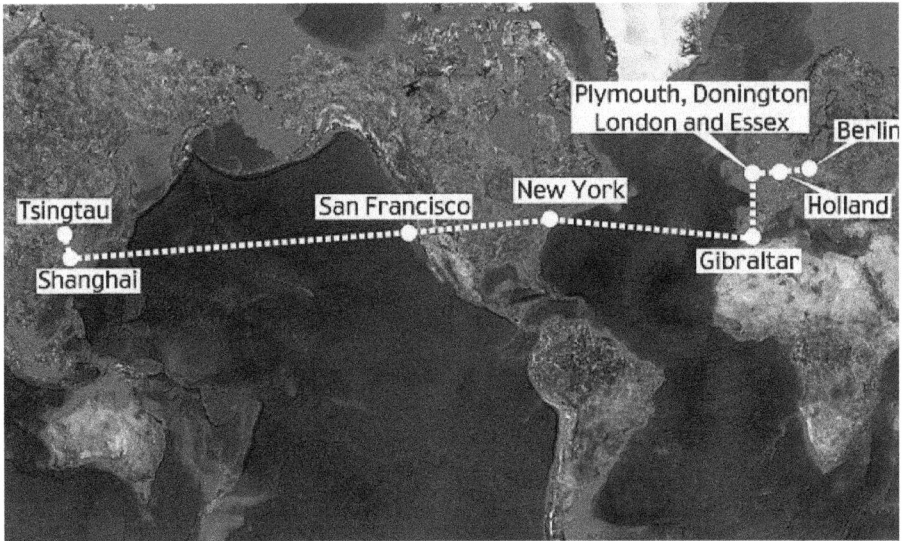

Gunther Plüschow's Route

Gunther was sharing a putrid cabin with three other men. The Frenchman on the top bunk was continually vomiting and the drunken Englishman smoked his pipe all day. The porthole could not be opened so all in all it was very unpleasant.

The final straw was the infestation of cockroaches!

The seas were rough and the ship pitched severely. The only respite for Gunther was the third class deck. It was from here that he spotted a German officer whom he had met in Shanghai. They had been in regular contact in New York and now here he was on the first class deck, having a great time. He managed to talk to his comrade and discovered his guise was that of a wealthy Dutchman. They were both travelling to Naples although their level of comfort differed greatly.

The ship's doctor suspected that Gunther had contracted malaria and so he was confined to his cabin for the duration of the voyage to Gibraltar. What irony!

Gibraltar was a British stronghold and the security was very tight. When they docked, non-English passengers weren't allowed to leave the ship. A boarding party arrived, led by British officer and twelve sailors. The Gibraltar police were also present.

The first class passengers were processed quickly and allowed to disembark. The grungy third class passengers however were treated differently.

When the time came for the Swiss passengers to be questioned, Gunther felt quietly confident having had a professionally forged passport and reasonable knowledge of the language.

Plüschow thought he had passed the test and he would be allowed to disembark. However, a man dressed in civilian clothes and reputed to be with the "Thomas Cook" agency insisted they all be thoroughly searched. When Gunther was searched it was discovered there were no clothing labels on any of his garments.

'This man is a German spy,' he shouted.

The officer requested one of the Swiss first class passengers be summoned to determine if these so-called 'Swiss' passengers had the correct accent.

Plüschow failed the test miserably.

'Excuse me Sir, my accent may not be perfect but I have an explanation.'

'Yes, and what is it?'

'I was born in Switzerland but my family moved to Italy when I was very young.'

'OK, let's hear you speak Italian.'

Gunther spoke fluently and with the correct accent, no hint of German.

The British officer wasn't convinced. Gunther was permitted to collect his belongings and was escorted off the ship. The prisoners were transferred onto a small naval vessel to be taken back to the garrison. As he looked longingly back at the ship he saw the wealthy Dutch gentleman standing on the deck. Gunther reflected on his situation; he had escaped the Japanese at Tsingtao, survived a crash landing in China and escaped from house arrest in Nanking. He had made his way across the United States and boarded a neutral ship, even surviving the third class voyage. Now he thought, 'some little arsehole travel agent had spotted that his suit had no labels, for God's sake!'

Once the Swiss party landed, they were marched up the rock by six soldiers and the officer who had boarded the ship. After an hour of marching through Gibraltar's streets they arrived at the military police station. They were all to be interviewed and when Gunther's turn came, he was quite indignant.

'Where is the Swiss consul? I demand that he be present throughout the interview.'

'I am afraid he won't be present. He is quite exhausted representing Swiss nationals. It would seem the entire Swiss population has passed through Gibraltar since the beginning of the war!'

Gunther was then searched, as were all the Swiss nationals.

'Have you any money?'

'No.'

The soldier started to frisk Plüschow; he came across a US twenty dollar coin.

'What's this?'

'Oh, I forgot I had that.'

'Did you?

The guard continued the search and found another twenty dollar coin and, worst of all, a small "Browning" revolver.

Gunther Plüschow was not going anywhere: he would not be seeing the consul and he certainly wasn't re-boarding the "Duca delgi Abruzzi."

He and the other Germans were marched off to their quarters. To greet them were fifty German civilians who had been interned at the start of the war.

They were all put to work hauling sacks of coal and fetching water. This was very hard work and Gunther had hardly lowered himself on the hard bunk, when he was asleep. He had virtually forgotten it was his twenty-ninth birthday.

Rule Britannia

Chapter 10

Soldiers yelling rudely awakened the detainees banging sticks on the doors; it was 4am.

They all had to be ready in twenty minutes they were sailing for England.

All the German prisoners were marched down to the dock, one prisoner started to sing "Die Wacht am Rhein" (The Watches on the Rhine) all started to sing this patriotic song until they reached the British troop ship.

Gunther and the other men were led to the cargo deck that had been petitioned. There were hammocks and a few tables and chairs. The latrine was on the upper deck; all prisoners were escorted when using the toilet. Gunther thought his cabin was awful on the "Duca delgi Abruzzi" but that was luxury compared to the living conditions he and his German compatriots had to endure on this ship.

The ten day voyage he and his fifty ship mates experienced, encompassed constant sea sickness and dysentery with a constant stream going up the ship's ladder to the deck under heavy guard and only one at a time to use the solitary bucket.

On the tenth day at sea the ship docked at Plymouth, Gunther Plüschow disembarked not as Ernst Suse the Swiss Locksmith but as a prisoner of war.

British soldiers loaded the prisoners onto a train and they were transported to Portsmouth. Once they had all been accounted for they were marched of to the local gaol. Conditions were sparse, cold and damp and they hadn't eaten all day. Gunther was able to bribe two old soldiers with yet another coin he had sewn into the hem of his suit coat.

The two veterans returned with all the provisions the prisoners needed including beer. They also brought firewood so in quick time they were sitting in front of the fire eating bread, cheese and corned beef and washing it down with beer. Things were looking up.

Despite the size of the camp beds and the firmness of the mattresses they were all able to get a good nights sleep.

The next morning the internees were taken to their new home, the "Andania" a merchant vessel which was leased by the British Government for ten thousand pounds a month to house POWs. Conditions on the ship were harsh. Gunther had revealed to the authorities his true status being a German officer he demanded his own cabin alas, his demands fell on deaf ears.

The greatest problem for the prisoners was boredom; reveille was at 6am, lights out at 10pm with nothing to occupy them in between..

The prison Governor did offer Gunther and his comrades vastly improved conditions if a bribe of one pound a day each was paid. The Governor's offer was declined.

Finally, Gunther and about thirty other Germans were transferred to a steamer and taken a shore. A train journey awaited them; anything was better than the prison ship.

The thirty Germans arrived in the village of Dorset from there they were marched off to a POW camp which was a converted army barracks. The conditions were quite spartan each hut contained thirty straw mattresses laid out on the floor and two thin blankets to protect the prisoners from the bitterly cold weather.

Gunther was pleasantly surprised the food was good and in abundance. Treatment by the prison guards was fair and playing sport was encouraged. Despite the conditions, Gunther continued to push the point that he should be located in an officer's camp. While being imprisoned at Dorset he received a letter from home informing him that his little sister, Carlotta had died, she was only twenty-three; Gunther was devastated; she was his best friend.

Shortly after hearing of Carlotta's death he received word that he was to be transferred to officer's camp. He bid farewell to his newly made friends, all German foot soldiers. The camp commandant, Major Owen came down to the railway station to see him off, Gunther was moved by the gesture.

Plüschow sat in a carriage alone and contemplated what may lay ahead. The train pulled into the station, the sign on the platform indicated they had arrived at Maidenhead just twenty-five miles west of London. A motorcar transported him to Holyport. A late Victorian walled mansion became his new home. It housed one hundred German officers and another forty orderlies to take care of the officers.

Gunther was escorted to his quarters, which held eight officers each with a proper bed and crisp white sheets. This was a huge improvement on the straw mattresses on the floor, which he had to try and sleep on for the past two months.

Life at Holyport was luxury compared to what he had endured on the ship and the Dorset camp the food was excellent and beer and wine was permitted. They had access to reading rooms, which were well stocked with German books.

Officers could also move around the grounds until lights out at 10pm.

Plüschow met some very well know Germans in the camp including Dr Martin Luther, Ferninand Friedensburg, the engineer who was instrumental in building the Panama Canal and world famous astronomer Dr Arnold Kohlschutter.

However, all good things must come to an end, Plüschow and the other German officers were informed that they were being moved to Donington Hall, a facility rumoured to be a luxury establishment suitable for the wealthy elite. A number of newspapers reported that the German officers were enjoying fox hunting and the local post office was having trouble coping with the volume of parcels arriving for the Donington inmates.

When Gunther and the other officers arrived at Donington they were very impressed.

There was a full guard, which presented arms and the officer in charge saluted.

They were then shown their quarters; he was pleased that he was to share with his very good friend, Fritz Siebel.

The stories of German officers being housed in a luxury manor house and partaking in various activities including hunting were totally false. The original four to a hut expanded to eight and the kitchens could not cope with the increase in the prisoner population. Donington had been allowed to deteriorate into not much more than a ruin. There were some redeeming features a twelfth century deer park and gardens were available to the prisoners and the roads and pathways winding through the one hundred year old oaks were delightful. Years later in the mid 1930's it became a motor raceway and the famous Dodington Raceway was born.

Cricket Match at Dodington Hall

Gunther would walk along the fence line pretending he was exercising but his true purpose was to find the weak link in which he could make his escape.

A faun had squeezed through the wire fence looking for its mother a few weeks before, if a faun could do it so could he!

The relationship between one of the old guards and Gunther had become quite close. Gunther didn't smoke so he would give the guard his allocation of cigarettes. In conversation Gunther asked him if he had ever left the camp for some entertainment.

'I go to the pictures in Derby every now and again.'

'How do you get all that way?'

'I ride my bicycle.'

'What! All that way, that's a long way a man of your age.'

'Are you calling me an old man! I can make it in under three hours!'

Gunther had just gleaned some of the information he needed for his escape plan.

Another time he asked the old guard in what direction Derby lay? Gunther told him that he was having a bet with another officer and the cigars in his hand were the guards if he could settle the bet.

'What direction did you say it was Plüschow?

'North.'

'You've won your bet!'

Gunther now had the information he needed the only other thing he required was a partner to escape with him.

Oskar Trefftz a German officer who had lived in England and spoke fluent English was chosen. Trefftz was a very willing accomplice and they set the date: Sunday, 4 July 1915.

Jail Break

Chapter 11

Gunther had been marched through the gates of Donington nine weeks before now he was planning to leave the crumbling estate by different means.

He and Oskar had rehearsed over and over again their escape now the day had arrived. That Sunday morning they both reported in sick. After roll call the sergeant checked their rooms, he found both men in bed looking very sick.

At 4pm they both got up and dressed, Gunther wore a sailor's uniform underneath a dark suit he had purchased in Shanghai. Stuffed in his pockets were all the things he thought he would need including a cap, razor and a knife. The knife was the most valuable possession which he was able to keep hidden from the guards. He also had strips of material; these would be used to protect his skin.

He also had six pounds borrowed from other prisoners. When he was able to pay them back God only knew.

One thing they were both lacking was forged papers or identity cards. Food was also scarce. Sneaking into the cabin of his old friend, Siebel, Gunther said farewell. Siebel hardly spoke English so it was out of the question that he be the one to accompany Plüschow.

The day had turned black with heavy rain sheeting down, Gunther, Oskar and Siebel walked outside onto the parade ground. If the British guards were wondering why three German officers were taking a stroll in such conditions they weren't showing it. All they cared about was finishing their watch and having a hot cup of tea and changing into dry uniforms!

The three entered the summerhouse; Siebel placed garden chairs around them and left in silence.

All Plüschow and Trefftz could do now was wait, they did not speak to each other they just sat there amongst the garden chairs in complete silence. The noise of the rain on the roof was deafening they could see out the windows and despite it being the middle of the day it was very dark. At least the British guards were not strolling around the gardens as they often did on a Sunday afternoon. Time was passing at a glacial rate then they heard the clock strike six. The bell rang for roll call now they would know if the first stage of their plan had worked.

The escapees were counting the seconds, their hearts were thumping and sweat was rolling down their faces. Thirty minutes had passed and no alarms had rung.

Both men had reported sick when the officer checked on them at evening roll call their comrades took their places running from hut to hut to ensure both beds were occupied. All seemed in order and the officer returned to his quarters until the final 10.30pm roll call.

Puschow and Trefftz still did not utter a sound. At 11pm there was a loud cheer from the POW's huts this was the signal to the two escapees that the officer had finished roll call and signed off as "present and accounted for."

They would not be missed until morning.

The change of the guard would be at 12 midnight it was time for the two of them to get up and stretch their legs, they went to the door and looked out. In the distance they could see the arc lamps illuminating the boundary fence and beyond; freedom!

Gunther crawled over to the section of the fence he had earlier identified as the weak point and signalled Trefftz to join him. No sentries could be seen. The first barbed wire fence was ten feet high with long spikes placed evenly every foot. They both wore leather leggings and leather gloves they also had material wrapped around their knees.

'We have to be careful not to touch the trip wire, if we do the bastards will be on us before we know it.

OK, I'll go first.' Gunther whispered to his comrade

Gunther started to climb the fence the protective clothing he had donned didn't seem to help much by the time he reached the other side he was bleeding badly.

Now it was Trefftz's turn, he too made it but with many cuts and blood oozing from his wounds. They both looked at each other; they said nothing, they just moved on to the next obstacle.

This was a barbed wire fence about three feet high and thirty feet wide.

'What do you reckon Gunther?'

'I think we just run through it, we can't get any more beaten up than we are now.'

Both of them threw themselves at the deadly obstacle and kept going until they reached the other side. Skin was hanging off their bodies they were both bleeding profusely but, they were alive!

Finally, they came to the third and final fence which was similar to the first with a trip wire, they made it over the top now they had to sneak past the guard house and onto the open road.

Gunther Plüschow in Escape Disguise

Both men carried a grey trench coat which they now wore having ditched the leggings and gloves. It was time to head for the village of Donington Castle. As the two escapees were striding down the road they saw a figure approaching from the opposite direction when they got closer they realised it was the sergeant-major from Donington

Hall. Trefftz quickly grabbed Plüschow and embraced him, the Sergeant Major simply walked past muttering 'bloody poofters.'

At a crossroad the sign "Derby" could be seen through the dim light now all they had to do was follow the road and head for the railway station. Once in London they would find a ship, which could take them to Europe and then Germany.

At dawn they arrived in Derby they found an isolated garden and shaved and tried to repair their clothes. Both donned collars and ties and tried to look respectable. The things they no longer needed were discarded. Nonchalantly the two men strolled down the London Road until they reached the Derby railway station.

The two escapees parted company agreeing to meet on the steps of St Paul's Cathedral once they had both reached London later that day.

Gunther arrived at St Pancras station and tried not to look nervous as the ticket collector glared at him. Striding out into London's bustling populace he merged into the throng.

By July 1915 Londoners had experienced the terrors of war up close and personal, the Kaiser had started to send his Zeppelins dropping bombs on the East End and the London Docks.

Bombing raids on London followed these raids with many civilians being killed and wounded. Londoners were shocked and angry and they took it out on any German citizens who were living in England despite many of them having lived there for many years. Therefore, London was not such a good place for Plüschow a German airman to be wandering around.

Visiting a number of restaurants Gunther was able to consume small portions so as not to draw attention to himself. Once nourished, he walked down to the Thames to try and ascertain how he would sneak aboard a ship to Europe. Disappointingly all the ships moored were heavily guarded and the neutral ships were all moored in the middle of the river.

Saint Paul's Cathedral was where he was to meet up with Oskar Trefftz at 7pm by 8pm he was starting to get worried and by 9pm it was obvious Oskar had either stowed away on a ship or had been captured.

Gunther headed back to the docks and decided he would try and get a meal and drink in one of the many pubs that lined the streets.

Cautiously he entered an old pub and ordered a pint of stout; they didn't have any food for sale. Sitting down in a booth the German tried to make it last until closing time. A cold beer from the homeland would have been his preference. When the pub closed its doors at 10pm Gunther knew he needed to find somewhere to sleep exhaustion was enveloping his whole being. Sauntering along the road trying not to look conspicuous he eventually came across an area with large impressive houses and beautiful gardens. The box hedge looked like a good place to hide and sleep. At 6am the sun was shining on his face it was time to get moving he started off down the road passing a policeman walking his beat. The bobby didn't give Plüschow a second glance. Eventually he entered Hyde Park where all the homeless were still sleeping on park benches. Still exhausted Gunther found a vacant bench and stretched out for some more sleep. Waking at 9am he looked around and discovered he was the last man sleeping. Rising from the hard bench Plüschow decided to head for a tube station to take him back to the dock area on his way he bought a newspaper. There was no mention of German POWs escaping on the front page but in the middle pages he saw the heading:

ESCAPES FROM DONINGTON HALL

ONE GERMAN OFFICER CAUGHT

AT

MILLWALL DOCKS; THE OTHER AT

LARGE

Two prisoners of war escaped Donington Hall yesterday morning and one of them named Treppitz was captured last evening at Millwall Docks.

The other, Gunther Plüschow by name, is still at large. His description is: height about 5ft 7ins, well-built, blue eyes, fair hair, fresh complexion, clean-shaven. He speaks English fairly well. So far as is known, he is wearing a mufti.

Gunther quite liked the description but knew he had to disguise himself or he would soon be back at Donington Hall.

Sauntering along the road so as not to bring attention to himself he discovered Blackfriars Station. The trench coat had to go, he approached the cloakroom and passed over the coat to the attendant.

'Name please?'

'Meinen.'

The attendant wrote down "Mr Mine"; he had a new identity although a cloakroom ticket was no substitute for proper identity papers.

Gunther got rid of his tie and collar and threw them in the bin he then rubbed coal dust, black shoe polish and Vaseline into his hair so he ended up with black greasy hair. This was a far cry from Gunther Plüschow German naval flying officer.

Staying out of harms way and avoiding contact with anyone was a priority. Keeping an eye on the shipping movements hoping to find a suitable neutral ship to sneak aboard was tantamount.

He bought "The Daily Mail" to see if they were still reporting the hunt for the dapper German officer.

"Gunther Plüschow, the German naval lieutenant fugitive from Donington Hall, has been at large seven days. The Chinese dragon tattooed on his left arm while serving in the east should however betray his identity."

The tattoo was well hidden under his sweater and ragged suit coat; he walked along with his hands in his pockets and spat a lot. He did not stand out from the crowd ambling along the docks.

Gunther was starting to believe he would never be able to stow away on a ship but a stroke of luck changed his thinking. He was on the top deck of a London bus just filling in the day when the two English gentlemen in the seat in front of him started up a conversation that took his interest. They were discussing a Dutch ship that dropped anchor at Tilbury in Essex every afternoon and departed at 7am for Flushing in the Netherlands. Exiting the bus he made his way back to

Blackfriars station an hour later he was standing on the dock at Tilbury. It was in the middle of the day when Gunther arrived, he decided he would go to a pub and get himself a hearty meal and a pint of ale.

He paid his 8d and was tucking into his lunch with the same table manners being displayed as the other wharfies sharing the table with him. He felt a tap on the shoulder; he froze. It was the publican he asked Gunther for his identity papers. He made the lame excuse that he had forgotten to put them in his pocket when he left for work that morning.

The publican instructed Gunther to remain seated, as he needed to make a telephone call. Gunther stared at the publican through the glass of the office talking intently to who ever it was on the other end of the line. He hoped it wasn't the police.

The publican returned.

'What's your name?'

'George Mine.'

'Where are you from?'

'America, my ship, the *Ohio*, has just berthed and I came in here for a meal and a pint; I've paid!'

'This is a private club only members can eat here. If you join you can come here as much as you like.'

Although Gunther had no intention of returning, he agreed and paid the three shillings membership fee. He was now a fully paid up member of the "Dockside Workingmen's Club".

His objective for the afternoon was to locate the Dutch steamer that would ferry him to Holland and then Germany. He lay on the banks of the river feigning sleep but actually watching all the ships coming and going. At last the ship he had been looking for flying the Dutch flag, the *Mecklenburg* started to slow and dropped anchor opposite where Gunther was sitting. His plan was to catch a ferry to Gravesend then take a barge out to the ship's buoy. The plan was to clamber up the hawser and find a secure hiding place. With luck he would be in Holland the next day.

He found a good spot to sleep amongst some timber and straw settling in for the night. He woke at midnight and crawled out of his cubby, he had trouble finding the barge he had selected earlier as it was now pitch black. Stumbling around he found it high and dry on the shore he hadn't taken into account the tides. He found a little dingy floating in the river and decided that would have to do. He started to wade out to it but the putrid mud made it extremely difficult he could hardly move at last he found the remnants of an old pier. Gunther pulled himself free he decided that would be enough for one night and made his way back to his cubby and immediately fell asleep.

He crawled out again at 7am just to see the *Mecklenburg* sailing down the river on her way to Holland. An opportunity missed. He spent the day eating in a dingy café on the dock and reading newspapers, naturally he had a particular interest in the stories about him. He was heading back to his hiding place when he saw another Dutch steamer moored in the river, the *SS Princess Juliana*.

Here was another chance! He decided this ship was going to take him to freedom.

He needed a new plan and a new spot to reach the ship; he selected a stony bank rather than the quagmire that almost took his life the previous night. He sat down on the banks and took off his boots and jacket. He pushed his razor and watch into his cap wading into the water he began to swim towards a rowing boat he had spotted from the shore. The river was bitterly cold he found it difficult to make any headway as the tide was going out and his clothes were weighing him down. The fast moving current was taking him down river and Gunther was too weak to fight it. Fortunately there was a sharp bend in the river and he was deposited on the shore. He rested on the bank for a while then he dragged himself to his feet and stumbled back to where his boots and coat were hidden. It was difficult putting them on but once on, he appreciated the relative comfort but he still trembled with the cold. He made it back to his hiding spot and tried to get some sleep but to no avail he was just too cold. Eventually when dawn broke he went into London and tried to dry off and seek some warmth sitting in the pews of a number of churches.

Once dry he found a cheap café and had a meal and continued his stroll until he came across a large crowd it was an army recruitment meeting! A large burly soldier came up to him and tried to coerce him into signing up to kill the bloody Krauts. Gunther made the excuse that he was American and couldn't leave his ship.

The next few days were spent visiting museums and music halls to try and relieve the boredom and get his strength back.

He knew he needed to reach the ship by stealing a small craft there was no way he would attempt swimming again. He found a dingy tied to the wharf, he lowered himself into the tiny vessel.

He reached for the oars only to find them padlocked fortunately the chains were quite loose and he managed to release them. He was a little concerned that the boat was taking in a small amount of water this grew progressively worse the dingy started to sink. He kept rowing as fast as he could when the boat came to an abrupt halt he had run aground on the same stinking mud that had almost engulfed him days before. He felt ridiculous sitting in a dingy high and dry in the river and going nowhere!

He was about four meters from the wharf; he knew he couldn't get out of the boat as he would sink into the slime. He devised a plan where he would use a boat hook to polevault himself towards the wharf knowing full well he was never going to make it.

He took off his boots and tied them around his neck he pole-vaulted himself out of the boat landing about two meters short of his target.

Once again, he found himself in the foul smelling mud; he struggled out and collapsed on the bank.

He made his way back to his cubby cold, muddied and dejected. The morning was cold and grey his clothes were both damp and caked in mud. He did his best to scrape the mud off and set out on a twenty-mile walk into central London. He spent his last pound on a ticket to a music hall to help him lift his spirits. Figuring he didn't need the money any longer as his intention was one last attempt and if that failed he would hand himself in and go back to Donington Hall.

The theme of the show was Britannia defeating an evil Germany, not the light entertainment he was hoping for he left the hall early. He made his way back to Gravesend Reach and discovered a small scull on the shore. Cutting it free he jumped in, pushing off with an ore however there were no rowlocks! He had to row the small craft like a canoe the river current soon took him down the river passing military pontoons and boats of all sizes and shapes. Steering the tiny vessel proved difficult he collided with the anchor rope of a coal tender. Gunther quickly wrapped a rope around the cable and moored the scull to the tender. He waited for dawn to break and cast off again letting the Thames take him. He was able to get the boat ashore at a bend in the river and it was here he rested for the next day and a half. The tide had turned and he cast off again heading up stream until he reached the coal tender once again he tied the boat to the anchor rope and waited. The Dutch ship was very close; at about 1am he cast off and started to paddle towards her he reached the ship's anchor buoy. He pushed the scull away with his foot and started to climb the steel cable clambering on board he saw the deck was deserted. Climbing on board he took off his boots, which he hid and began to investigate the ship. Approaching the cargo deck he hoped to find a suitable hiding place. Frozen in his tracks he saw two sentries on the deck and staring directly at him he moved back and waited but they obviously had not seen him. It was essential he find a hiding place he edged forward and reached the promenade where the majority of the lifeboats were located. The stowaway undid the ties and slipped under the cover and collapsed. He slept soundly only to be woken by the ship's siren announcing the ship's arrival at Flushing, Holland. He had made it! After all the pain and frustration over the past week

Climbing out of the lifeboat nobody paid any attention at all. The only acknowledgement was from the women passengers who turned up their noses at this dirty smelly vagabond.

Gunther put his hands firmly in his pockets and sauntered down the gangway and onto neutral safe soil.

He exited through a door marked "Entry Forbidden" and stepped out onto the dock.

Gunther boarded a train for Germany and although he was questioned a number of times including by the German authorities, he made it to Berlin.

He was heralded as "The Hero of Tsingtao" was promoted to Lieutenant Commander. and was put in charge of Kiel-Holtenau a significant naval air station. He married his sweetheart Isot and they had a son.

Gunter's and Isot's Wedding Day

He wrote a book "The Adventures of the Airman of Tsingtao" which became a best seller.

Gunther Plüschow deserves to be the first escapee to be honoured in this book.

Holzminden

Chapter 12

Holzminden Perimeter Fence

Every POW dreams of escape and that dream was even more intense at Holzminden; the punishment meted out by Niemeyer made the prisoners determined that they would escape this hellhole.

A plan was devised to tunnel out beyond the perimeter fence and into a rye field. The tunnel was to begin at the foot of the staircase in the orderlies' quarters, *Kaserne B*, which was the closest block to the fence.

All officers were strictly forbidden from entering the orderlies' quarters mainly due to the fact that this was the closest point to the perimeter fence. There were guards stationed directly opposite plus the guards manning the towers had a clear view. The problem they faced was exiting the officers' quarters walking along the exterior of the building and entering the orderlies' quarters. They overcame this problem by borrowing the orderly's uniforms and waiting for a signal from their own sentries (orderlies) that the coast was clear. This method worked well and they never had a problem getting into the place where the tunnel was being dug.

After several plans were rejected as being too risky including tunnelling past the punishment cells, a new plan was devised. There was an area next to the cellar stairs that had been barricaded off with very thick boards. It had been constructed as a security measure so prisoners could not hide and "jump" the guard on duty. The fact that it was next to the stairs would indicate that the void under the stairs would be adequate to be the tunnel entrance.

The only problem was the officers did not have any proper tools to pry the boards off and replace them neatly enough to avoid detection.

They devised a plan to break a door so that the prison had to call in a village carpenter to repair it. They knew that all his tools would be counted both before and after the work was completed. One of the officers started a verbal fight with the guard and while the wild ruckus was going on another officer stole the tools they needed. The guard discovered the theft immediately but no amount of searching could discover where they had been hidden. This put the guard in a dilemma: if he reported the theft he would be accused of dereliction of duty and locked away for some time in the punishment cells. He decided to "save his own skin" and keep his mouth shut. He paid the carpenter a bribe to purchase new tools.

The officers now had all the tools needed for the job, they decided to remove the boards between 12noon and 3pm as this was when the camp took its siesta and all apart from the guards on duty would disappear including Commandant Niemeyer.

While two officers kept watch another two started to remove the boards, this was not an easy task, as they had to complete it in total silence so as not to alert the guards.

They managed to remove all the boards and to their delight, found the space to be about four yards by five and the ceiling height was just less than six feet. This would be a perfect spot to start their tunnel to freedom.

They had to replace the boards and incorporate a door which could not be detected once this was completed they returned to their own quarters.

Every day from then on the tunnelling team went to room twenty-four, changed into their orderlies' uniforms. There were a number of scouts placed strategically around the camp to keep a lookout and give the "all clear' signal to the tunnelers.

The officers would then make their way along the building and enter the orderlies' quarters to begin their tunnelling shift.

When day's digging was complete they would use the same methodology to return to their own quarters. If there were guards in close proximity, other officers or orderlies would distract them with conversation or some pretext.

Although there were a few close calls including Niemeyer coming to the building next to the orderlies' quarters while they were digging. Overall, all went well throughout the months of tunnelling.

The code of secrecy was absolute; tunnelers would not divulge what they were doing to their fellow officers in the next bunk let alone the others sharing the hut. There may have been suspicions but nobody knew what exactly was going on.

The tunnelling process was taking a long time; their hours of work were very much restricted by the camp regime of roll call and the issue of the daily potato ration from the adjoining cellar. Work therefore could not begin until after 11am and end well before the 4pm roll call.

The tunnelers worked in almost complete darkness and the smell, which greeted them each day, was putrid; stale air, dampness and sweat.

The worst part was putting on their damp wet mud encrusted digging clothes, which was worn in the tunnel.

They encountered a number of obstacles that could have proved to be fatal to the tunnel's completion but ingenuity and hard work overcame them.

The final obstacle was the building's foundation, which were constructed with concrete and sitting on solid rock. In a normal situation one would use a jackhammer and bolt cutters to break through the steel reinforcing. The tunnelers only had kitchen knives, spoons, penknives and anything else they could find to tunnel. There was a cold chisel from the stolen carpenter's tools, which did help, but it was not going to complete the task.

One thing they had learned from living in Germany was fifty marks could buy you most things. They bribed a village workman who was working in the camp to supply some sulphuric acid. Fashioning some clay cups enabled them to pour the acid on the steel reinforcing rods, which melted the rods allowing them through.

Once through the foundations they turned north heading for the perimeter fence and out past the prison grounds to the rye field. It was essential they came up in the field and not open ground as the guards would spot them with the aid of their searchlights; the escapees would be sitting ducks.

The tunnel was not much more than a rabbit hole, it was sixteen inches wide and twelve inches high; the tunnelers had to wriggle through, certainly not crawl. There was no other way to dig, as the amount of earth extracted had to be limited as it all had to be hidden in the cellar. Each digger was allocated one candle as they were very hard to obtain, each man had to move along in pitch black until they reached their allotted location and then light the candle and begin digging.

As in any man made tunnel it had to be reinforced with timber planks all of which were stolen. These came not only from the tunnelers beds but other POWs in the hut also. Many a complaint was made including by the tunnelling team but the mystery of the missing boards was never solved.

Once the boards had been seconded and were in the tunnel, they had to be secured which was an exhausting process. They had to be cut to the right size as the measurements differed along the tunnel. A tunneler would drag a board along the tunnel to the point where it was required. He would have to roll on his back holding the board in place with one hand and with the other hand wedge an upright board under one end to brace it. Nothing was easy about tunnelling out of Holzminden.

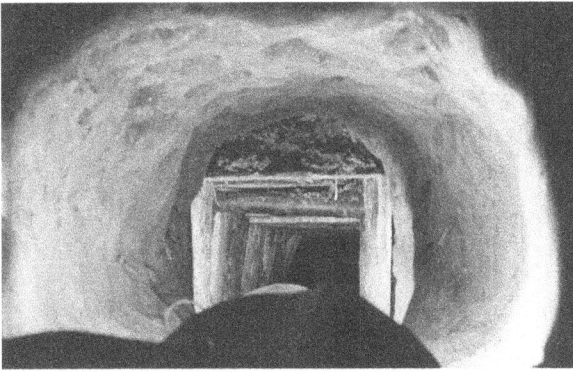

Holzminden Escape Tunnel

When a tunneler had filled his soil bowl he would lift himself up as far as the twelve-inch ceiling of the tunnel would allow and pass it under his body. He would then tug on the rope to signal to the man at the end of the tunnel to haul it out. The soil would be shovelled into pillowcases stolen from the living quarters and stacked against the cellar walls. When the cellar was full they hauled the bags up to the attic or filled their pockets and stored it under the roof tiles.

At the end of the day at 3.45pm, the three man digging team had to be out of the tunnel. They changed back into their orderlies' uniforms and returned in the same manner as they arrived in the morning with scouts looking out for guards and their mates manning the doors. Once inside their quarters they changed into their normal uniforms.

The 4pm roll call came and went without incident.

As they were nearing the completion of the tunnel Commandant Niemeyer had grown suspicious of an escape and increased the number of guards outside the perimeter fence with one stationed directly over the spot where the tunnel would emerge.

Colonel Rathborne, the senior officer, decided to dig another tunnel off the main tunnel heading north instead of west, which was the original route. This would require them to dig a much longer tunnel to reach the rye crops they needed for cover.

They were required to dig another fifty meters to reach the rye but progress was slow as rocks and roof collapses were slowing their pace down to two feet a day. The supply of timber boards was also slowing up so they were forced to take risks.

They were racing against time as the rye crop was due to be harvested in early August and they couldn't afford to lose their cover.

Break Out

Chapter 13

At last the tunnel was complete, it was decided that one of the officers, Lieutenant Butler, would make his way to the end of the tunnel dig up until he broke the earth and wave a little white flag for two seconds. The officers in the barracks would keep watch and identify where exactly the tunnel exit would be.

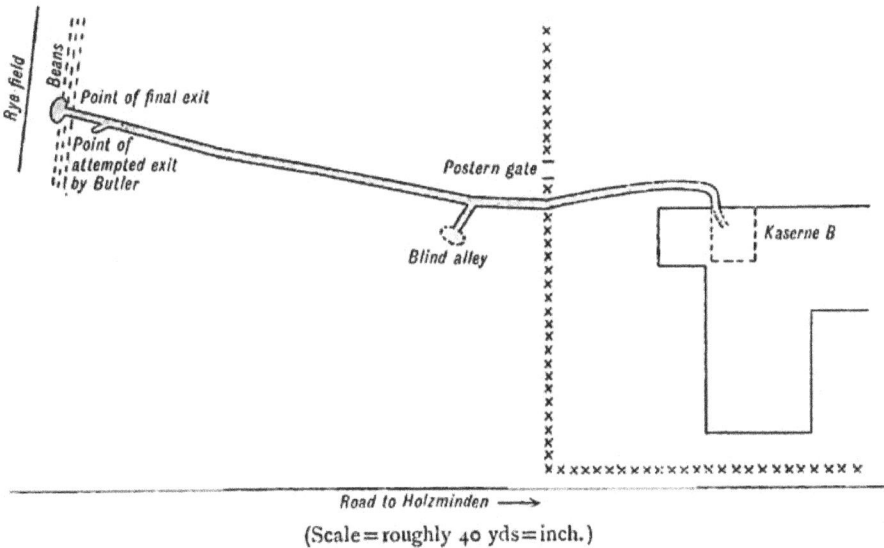

(Scale = roughly 40 yds = inch.)

The officers watched in horror as the flag was waved in a bean field ten yards short of the rye. There was little chance they could dig the extra distance before the rye was harvested so they decided to work with what they had. The beans did give some protection although not as much as their original target.

The night of the escape arrived at last; there was excitement and tension in *Kaserne A* as the men of the tunnelling team prepared to enter the tunnel. None of the men were told their allocated sequence so as not to create too much tension and excitement. They were instructed to go to bed fully clothed and be ready to go when they were tapped on the shoulder.

The final barracks inspection was at 10pm both barrack doors were then locked.

The escapees had to climb through a hole cut in the attic of the officers' quarters and crawl along the ceiling eaves until they reached the trapdoor in the orderlies' section. An Australian Lieutenant, Louis Grieve, was working as the "doorman' at the hole in the attic. He would not permit the next man to pass through until he received word that the last man had passed through the tunnel entrance.

Grieve was a big burly man so no one was going to argue with him.

The first man to exit the tunnel was Lieutenant Butler, he was allocated the task of "breaking out" he used a bread knife that had been stolen from the kitchen to dig out a six inch hole large enough for him to stick his head out and observe the lay of the land. He was delighted to discover the exit was in the middle of the bean field and not far from the rye.

The arc lights illuminated the perimeter fence and beyond. He heard a cough and quickly looked in that direction it was a guard.

Butler was out of the light so he hoped he had been spotted. He waited for a minute but the guard had not moved. He spent the next thirty minutes widening the exit hole and then pushed his escape kit out and made for the rye field. He noticed that not far away was a guard snoring; obviously sound asleep. He was oblivious to the fact there was a major escape happening right under his nose.

The other two men in Butler's group were Langren and Clouston, they exited the tunnel soon after Butler. It was 11.45pm and the heavy rain that had been falling throughout the night had ceased. There was a full moon and it now started to shine through the clouds. The increased light together with the fact that the rye was now ripe making a loud crackling noise when touched did not improve their chances of getting away undetected.

It was decided to make their way through the beans until they reached a point where they needed to cross a large field. Just then, it started to rain again quite heavily and the noise of the rain on the rye allowed them to proceed without being heard. At the far side of the field they stopped to put on their rucksacks and looked back at Holzminden; they all hoped for the last time.

Reaching the river they discovered a raft; loading it up with their rucksacks and their clothing they pushed it across the river. The three men then made off in a north-westerly direction heading for the Dutch frontier.

While Butler and his comrades were making good their escape, the rest of the escapees were working their way through the tunnel and crawling into the beans and other crops. Most of them were in groups of three.

The escapees went off in different directions, some even moving east towards Berlin to confuse the Germans. The officers who spoke fluent German chose to travel by train speeding up their exit from the enemy territory.

The original thirteen man tunnelling team were now through the tunnel, it was now the turn of Colonel Rathborne and six supplementary officers. He was a portly man and found it extremely difficult to get through the tunnel with his kit being pushed in front; he made it. The other six entered the tunnel every few minutes with the last man out being James Bennett. All up, twenty-nine had been able to traverse the tunnel and make their escape.

Lieutenant Cecil Blain, Captain David Gray and Lieutenant Caspar Kennard

All three made it to freedom wearing these outfits.

Escape Tunnel Discovered

The thirtieth man was not so fortunate, the tunnel collapsed in on him and the man behind had to drag him out. The tunnel was inspected and the decision was reluctantly taken that there would be no more escapes that night. The remaining prisoners, fifty in all, had to return to their beds bitterly disappointed and not looking forward to the morning when roll call was taken; they knew retribution that would be taken. The tunnel was closed and the secret hatches and doors sealed so the guards would not find them in their search. In the mad rush to exit the tunnel by 6am they had to leave two escapees until the roll call had been completed. Once freed, they raced back to their barracks not by the safe route but straight out the door of the orderlies' quarters. They ran into Niemeyer conducting an impromptu inspection, he questioned them both but did not ask them why their uniforms were so soiled. Just then, Niemeyer heard local farmers yelling to him from the other side of the perimeter fence. He approached them to hear their grievances, they were angry about their crops being crushed and trampled. This sent alarm bells ringing in Niemeyer's head he demanded the gates be opened and he and several guards went to inspect the damage. It was easy to discover the exit hole and Niemeyer ordered a guard to enter the tunnel and trace it back to its source. The guard refused not willing to take the risk of discovering escapees still in the tunnel. He placed a guard at the exit hole and returned to camp to report the escape to his superiors in Hanover. He dispatched one of his men to complete a headcount the guard returned and reported twenty-nine missing. Niemeyer's jaw dropped, he turned grey it seemed he had aged ten years in that very instant. He then began to yell and rant in a ridiculous manner, you could hear the laughter emanating from the prisoners barracks.

Niemeyer immediately ordered all doors to be locked and issued "safety of camp" orders, all prisoners were confined to barracks and their rooms with all communication between prisoners banned. He also issued orders to his guards that if they saw anybody at the windows, to shoot them! This actually happened when he spotted an officer looking out. He ordered a guard to shoot narrowly missing he officer and shattering the window. There were more shots fired at the building and one prisoner received a flesh wound from a bayonet; all in all total chaos! One of the officers rigged up a dummy attached to a rope, which could be moved up and down in front of the window. There was much firing of rifles and shattering of glass and laughter inside the barracks.

For the next month life inside the camp was "hell on earth" for the prisoners, the punishment cells were full of officers incarcerated for doing nothing and beatings became a regular occurrence. The local villagers hearing about the escape would gather outside the fence as though they were an audience at a circus. This infuriated Niemeyer even more, he believed they were mocking him.

He instituted new procedures where guards would inspect inside the barracks three times a night shining a bright torch into each prisoner's eyes. Sleep deprivation became a real issue.

If these conditions were not bad enough "Spanish Flu" was sweeping throughout Germany and the rest of the world. Several officers died from the pandemic although other camps suffered up to one thousand deaths.

In the meantime, the escapees were all making their way to the Dutch border some hiding for twenty-one hours and only travelling in the dead of night for the remaining three. With the aid of home-made compasses and a map smuggled into the camp from England they managed to find their way. An Australian officer who had been a photographer before the war duplicated the map. He managed to bribe locals with food from Red Cross parcels for photographic equipment. Each team had a copy of this very detailed map.

Of the twenty-nine who escaped, ten made it to Holland and their freedom, the nineteen who were recaptured were all tried and convicted; they were sentenced to six months imprisonment in a civilian gaol. Because the Armistice was close their sentences was never enforced.

Even after the "great escape" prisoners were attempting to break out of the camp; another tunnel had been dug. William Leefe Robinson was one of the 'would be' escapees. Unfortunately Robison suffered from acute claustrophobia and half way through the tunnel he suffered a panic attack and started screaming. The guards heard the noise and uncovered the tunnel.

Robinson was getting used to the punishment cells and that is where he ended up again. The war ended soon after and Robinson was shipped home only to die of "Spanish Flu" soon after arriving home. A sad ending to Britain's hero, a Victoria Cross recipient, the first man to bring down a Zeppelin.

The First Doughboy to Escape the Germans

Frank Savicki

Chapter 14

"Doughboy" is the term given to American soldiers in the First World War, later in World War Two; they were called G.I.s (Government Issue).

Frank Savicki, a coal miner from Pennsylvania, was the first American prisoner of War to escape from a German camp.

Emigrating from Poland prior to the Great War in 1910 he became an American citizen in 1916. Frank and his sister Anna lived with their uncle and Frank began his time at the mine as a mule driver.

In April 1917 he enlisted in the American Expeditionary Force, A.E.F. a few weeks after America entered the war.

Savicki was small even by 1917 standards but he was strong and wiry; he was five feet four inches tall.

His Division, the 28th was dubbed "The Iron Division" for its toughness and endurance in battle. The 28th Division fought at Champagne Marne and Meuse-Argonne as well as a number of smaller battles.

The Meuse-Argonne Offensive was arguably the bloodiest battle in American history. During the Meuse-Argonne battle the American Expeditionary Force fired off more ammunition than had the Union side during the entire American Civil War.

In June 1918 Russia was defeated and had surrendered to the Germans, Paris looked very vulnerable. But things can change very quickly in war; despite the long succession of Allied defeats in the summer of 1918 the allies were able to successfully counter attack. Battles in east of Verdun and in the St-Mihiel salient, which was the first major solo offensive by the US army, started to turn failure into success. These individual operations were fought from 26-28

September in a co-ordinated assault all along the Western Front from Flanders to the Argonne.

Unlike 1915 and 1917, the allies were successful in controlling the air and the sea. The Turks were also defeated in the east.

Germany had planned an organised withdrawal but General Ludendorff believed it would be seen as a retreat and would weaken precarious public confidence and the resolve of their dwindling military forces.

However, the Germans had no real choice as the Allies combined new and effective tactics with fresh American reinforcements, this forced the Germans back. The senseless slaughter seen at the Somme where men and resources were repeatedly thrown at the same objective was changed. A strategy of short surprise attacks which were suspended before enemy reinforcements could be called were employed. Germany was forced to adopt a new strategy of tactical retreat with sporadic counter-attacks in the hope of persuading the Allies to negotiate a reasonable peace.

As part of the Allied push forward Marshal Foch, the French commander, asked the Americans to concentrate on the Meuse-Argonne area. The American attack on the forested hills of St Mihiel had seen over half a million Americans and over one hundred thousand French force a German withdrawal in just over a day. Such success helped the Allies believe that even the Hindenburg Line was going to be an easy objective. The Americans would attack on 26 September in the Meusse Argonne area as part of a much larger push along the whole front.

The quick and decisive win at St Mihiel was not to be repeated. On 26 September, American commander John Pershing sent his men through the 'formidable' terrain of the Meusse-Argonne battlefield and up against entrenched German defences. Pershing believed that speed and the sheer weight of superior numbers would secure him another decisive victory.

At first the Americans under cover of fog, made surprisingly good progress. But soon the German machine guns occupying the high ground combined to slow the American attack to a standstill. Supply lines were stretched to the limit; American soldiers were fighting with no food in their bellies. It took another two weeks of fierce fighting before they reached the eastern section of the Hindenburg Line. Finally, after forty-seven days, and with over twenty six thousand Americans dead the Meusse attack ended on 11 November, what we now know as Armistice Day.

"Frank Savicki had been involved in these battles, and was one of the few to survive. He was discovered by the Germans hiding in a shell hole and taken prisoner. After questioning he was sent to a secure farmhouse where he was locked away for two days in darkness without food or water. The Germans stripped him of his personal possessions including his watch and razor and the little money he had in his pockets.

On the third day he began a two-day march to a prison camp at Laon, guarded by two German soldiers.

On arrival at the camp weak from fatigue and hunger, Savicki was put in prison barracks in which were quartered several hundred other Americans, French, British, and Italians. The barracks had been converted from some large public buildings and was surrounded by a barbed wire fence.

Savicki spent six weeks in the Laon prison camp. He noted, "There were several hundred prisoners, about fifty of whom were Americans. We worked every day from seven o'clock in the morning until eight or nine o'clock at night. We were divided into small gangs of six to twelve to work on the roads, on the railroads, or unloading supplies."

Laon P.O.W. Camp

Rations were sparse: *'every morning we were given our bread ration - three pounds for seven men. At morning and at night we were given a can of so-called coffee. At noon we were given soup made of some kind of grass and horsemeat. There never was much meat in it, though. This noonday issue was the only pretence of a meal of the whole day. Frank Savicki*

Living conditions were horrific: "There were no beds in the barracks and none of us had blankets. We slept on the barn floor. There was cold water in the yard, but no means for taking a bath. No one had a change of clothes and there was no means of washing those we had. In all the month and a half I was at Laon I did not have my clothes off. Everybody was covered with lice."

After six weeks in Laon, Savicki was moved again, to Rastatt, in Baden. He made the trip in a boxcar with forty-odd other Americans.

The journey took three days and two nights during which they subsisted on one piece of bread each and two drinks of water

Two weeks were spent at Rastatt where conditions were better than at Laon: a shower bath had been shipped from Switzerland. Savicki got a bath and a change of underwear. He remained fifteen days in this camp and received two boxes from the Red Cross, each containing ten pounds of canned meat, beans, tobacco, and hard tack.

Based at the Rastatt camp, Savicki worked seven days a week on a farm owned by an elderly German man and his wife. He was quartered in a guardhouse with a number of Russian P.O.W.'s. It was they who showed him a distant mountain over the border in Switzerland. Originally from Russia, Savicki spoke the language; the POWs all soon became friends. They spoke about the possibilities of escape; some of them had been captives for nearly four years.

After two weeks on the farm, he decided to make a break for Switzerland.

Frank was able to deceive the guard by hiding in the guardhouse and then made his escape

A newspaper report describes Savicki's journey:

"He cut straight across country avoiding all highways. His path lay over the tops of several hills, through knots of woods and stretches of ground heavy with underbrush across several small-cultivated valleys. He travelled all night guided by the knob of the mountain. He paused when he saw before him, glistening in the moonlight, a little river, which he knew separated Germany from Switzerland.

Dawn found him in a clump of shrubbery on a hillside less than three hundred yards from the nearest sentry boxes scarcely more than one hundred feet apart along the international boundary. In the cover of the bushes he remained all day. Before him, he could see the river and the difficulties before him in crossing it."

119

The difficulties were barbed wire, railroad tracks, and the river itself.

Savicki noticed that the guards stayed in their boxes, it must have been too comfortable for them and therefore they didn't patrol. The river was too broad to jump so he decided to try vaulting it. Finding a suitable branch he shaped it into the right shape to use for a vaulting pole.

The newspaper report continues, "After dark, he started crawling slowly and cautiously. The trip to the edge of the barbed wire took five or six hours. He came to the railroad track and crawled over. He reached the edge of the river. He stood on the bank. The other bank ten feet away was Switzerland and safety. He poised his vaulting pole and sprang for the further side. The pole sank four feet into the mud of the river bottom. Private Frank Savicki landed belly deep in the water with something of a splash.

There was a tense minute. Clinging to a clump of grass on the Swiss bank, Savicki waited for the bullets he was certain were coming. But none came. Evidently the Boche had not heard him. Finally, he pulled himself onto the land. He was a prisoner no more.

By daylight he made a little Swiss village in which he met an old man who dried his clothes before a fireplace and gave him breakfast. The town received him graciously and bought him a railway ticket to Berne. At Berne the Red Cross fitted him out in a new uniform and the American colony outdid itself in affording entertainment worthy of an American ex-prisoner from Germany."

Frank survived the remainder of the war.

Colditz

Chapter 15

Colditz Castle Photo Taken 1945

Colditz Castle is a Renaissance castle in the town of Colditz near Leipzig, Dresden and Chemnitz in the state of Saxony in Germany. The castle was used as a workhouse for the poor. It was also home for the mentally sick for over 100 years. It became the most famous Prisoner of War prison during the Second World War housing the "incorrigible" Allied officers who had repeatedly escaped from other camps.

The castle lies between the towns of Hartha and Grimma on a spur over the Zwickauer Mulde and had the first wildlife park in Germany.

In 1046, Henry III of the Holy Roman Empire gave the burghers of Colditz permission to build the first documented settlement at the site. In 1083, Henry IV urged Margrave Wiprecht of Groitzsch to develop the castle site, which Colditz accepted. In 1158, Emperor Frederick Barbarossa made Thimo I "Lord of Colditz", and major building works began. By 1200, the town around the market was established. Forests, empty meadows, and farmland were settled next to the pre-existing Slavic villages Zschetzsch, Zschadraß, Zollwitz, Terpitzsch and Koltzschen. Around that time the larger villages Hohnbach, Thierbaum, Ebersbach and Tautenhain also emerged.

In the Middle Ages, the castle played an important role as a lookout post for the German Emperors and was the centre of the Reich territories of the Pleißenland (anti-Meißen Pleiße-lands). In 1404, the nearly 250-year rule of the dynasty of the Lords of Colditz ended when Thimo VIII sold Colditz Castle for 15,000 silver marks to the Wettin ruler of the period in Saxony.

Various renovations were completed through the Middle Ages, it was also rebuilt in 1504 when a fire which began in the bakery razed the castle to the ground.

In the 19th century, the church space was rebuilt in the neo-classic architectural style, but its condition was allowed to deteriorate. The castle was used by Frederick Augustus III, Elector of Saxony as a workhouse to feed the poor, the ill, and persons under arrest. It served this purpose from 1803 to 1829, when its workhouse function was taken over by an institution in Zwickau. In 1829, the castle became a mental hospital for the "incurably insane" from Waldheim. In 1864, a new hospital building was erected in the Gothic Revival style, on the ground where the stables and working quarters had been previously located. It remained a mental institution until 1924.

The castle was home to several notable figures during its time as a mental institution, including Ludwig Schumann, the second youngest son of the famous composer Robert Schumann and Ernst Baumgarten, one of the original inventors of the airship.

When the Nazis came to power in 1933, they turned the castle into a political prison for communists, homosexuals, Jews and other "undesirables". Beginning in 1939 allied prisoners was housed there.

After the outbreak of World War II the castle was converted into a high security prisoner-of-war camp for officers who had become security or escape risks or who were regarded as particularly dangerous. Since the castle is situated on a rocky outcrop above the River Mulde, the Germans believed it to be an ideal site for a high security prison.

The larger outer courtyard, known as the Kommandantur, had only two exits and housed a large German garrison. The prisoners lived in an adjacent courtyard in a ninety-foot (twenty seven meter) tall building. Outside, the flat terraces which surrounded the prisoners' accommodation were constantly watched by armed sentries and surrounded by barbed wire. Although known as Colditz Castle to the locals, its official German designation was Oflag IV-C and it was under Wehrmacht control.

Although it was considered a high security prison, it boasted one of the highest records of successful escape attempts. This could be owing to the general nature of the prisoners that were sent there; most of them had attempted escape previously from other prisons and were transferred to Colditz because the Germans had thought the castle escape-proof.

In April 1945, US troops entered Colditz town and, after a two-day fight, captured the castle on 16 April. In May 1945, the Soviet occupation of Colditz began. Following the Yalta Conference it became a part of East Germany. The Soviets turned Colditz Castle into a prison camp for local burglars and non-communists. Later, the castle was a home for the aged and nursing home, as well as a hospital and psychiatric clinic. For many years after the war, forgotten hiding places and tunnels were found by repairmen, including a radio room set up by the British POWs, which was then "lost" again only to be re-discovered some ten years later.

Barbed-wire
Flood lights

Note:- Solid parts of Castle prepared from an MS of the Seventeenth Century

STEEP DROP

Road to Park

GERMAN KOMMANDANTUR

Terrace

Raised catwalk with patrolling sentry

Parapet

Flower bed

Path

Sentry

Gate in Archway

Gate in barbed wire

Grass Area

MOAT

STEEP DROP

Cells for Prominent

Dentist

CANTEEN

Store Shed

Sentry

Grass Lawn

Sentry with Machine gun

Sentry with Machine gun in roof by night

PRISONER'S KITCHEN

GERMAN KITCHENS

CHAPEL

INNER COURTYARD (PRISONERS)

Sentry

Sentry

Delousing Shed

OUTER COURTYARD (GARRISON)

Sentry

Clock Tower (Above)

MOAT BRIDGE

Gate Sentry

Clothes Store

Office

Down to Cellars

Light

Shower baths

ORDERLIES QUARTERS (Above)

Light-well

Gate Sentry

PRECIPICE

Solitary Confinement Cells

SICK WARD

PARCELS OFFICE

THEATRE 3rd floor

SENIOR OFFICERS QUARTERS (Upper floors)

Gate

Sentry

ROUND TOWER

Sentry with Machine gun in roof by night

Terrace

Parapet

Sentry by day

GUARD HOUSE

Sentry

Entrance Gate RAMPART

Sentry

GERMAN QUARTERS (over road)

Solitary confinement cell

Garden (Orchard)

Sentry by night

Sentry by night

Sentry

Raised catwalk with patrolling sentry

Sentry with Machine gun in Pagoda

Sentry with Machine gun

Parapet

PRECIPICE

PRECIPICE

N

10 5 0   10   20 Yards

Reach for the Sky

Douglas Bader - Guest of Colditz

Douglas Bader was born in London, England on February 21, 1910. His father, Frederick Bader, was a civil engineer and his mother Jessie, played Mah-jong.

The first two years of young Doug's life was spent with relatives on the Isle of Man as his parents were living in India due to Fred's work commitments. Douglas joined his parents in India from the age of two until returning home to Britain a year later. The family settled

126

in London. In 1914 with the outbreak of World War I, Bader's father joined the military. Frederick was badly wounded in the Battle of Passchendaele in 1917 he was repatriated home but died as a result of his wounds in 1922.

Jessie did not grieve long and re-married soon after. She and her new husband did not want a little twelve year old getting in the way, he was sent to Saint Edward's School as a border.

His class had an excursion to the RAF College at Cranwell; Bader set his sights on becoming a pilot and won a place as a cadet at RAF College Cranwell.

Bader was commissioned as an Officer in the Royal Air Force in 1930 and was posted to 23 Squadron at RAF Kenley. Bader demonstrated great ability as a pilot in fact he was selected to fly in the Squadron's aerobatic display team at the prestigious RAF Hendon display in 1931.

His reputation for taking risks was well known particularly in low level aerobatics. In December 1931, Bader crashed during an unauthorized low-level aerobatic routine at Woodley while visiting the Reading Aero Club. He survived the crash although he came close to death. He had both his legs amputated.

Doctors fitted him with artificial "tin" legs soon, Bader learned to walk without the use of a stick and was not only driving his car but also flying.

Douglas was certified by the Central Flying School as perfectly able to fly however, the Air Force had no precedent to guide them, they could only offer him a ground based commission.

Bader resigned and found work with the Asiatic Petroleum Company.

Douglas didn't enjoy civilian life although he was happily married and was the only golfer with tin legs playing from a ten handicap at his club.

With the outbreak of the Second World War Bader applied to rejoin the RAF. With pilots in short supply they accepted his application by June 1940 Bader had been posted to command 242 Squadron, which had suffered badly in The Battle of France.

Bader and Friend From the 242

He knew he had to raise morale; Bader's methods were typically uncompromising. His management skills brought the 242 back into an effective fighting unit.

Bader made an impact on The Battle of Britain with his aggressive tactics and the determination of his squadron. He was promoted to Wing Commander in 1941 and was stationed at RAF Tangmere, he lead the "Tangmere Wing" in sweeps over North West Europe aimed to bring the Luftwaffe into combat. By the summer of 1941 Bader had claimed twenty two victories making him the fifth highest scoring pilot in the RAF.

Bader was flying over France in August 1941 when German fighters shot him down. Bader bailed out from his damaged machine and parachuted to the ground but both his artificial legs were badly damaged.

Bader was captured by German forces and was taken to a hospital near St Omer where his damaged artificial legs were repaired. The German hospital staff feeling sympathy for the legless pilot allowed Bader to retain his clothing. French villagers helped him break out from hospital! The locals escorted him to a farm but someone betrayed him and he was re-arrested. Taking no further chances, the Germans put Bader under close guard and he was sent to a Prisoner of War camp. Eventually he arrived at Colditz as a result of his constant and unremitting hostility to his captors. Bader remained in captivity despite numerous escape attempts until Colditz was liberated in 1945.

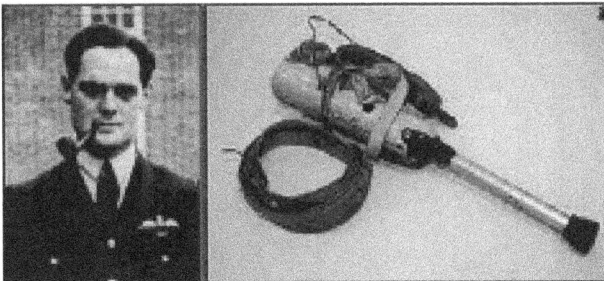

Bader and His Tin Leg

Billie Stephens Made a Home Run from Colditz

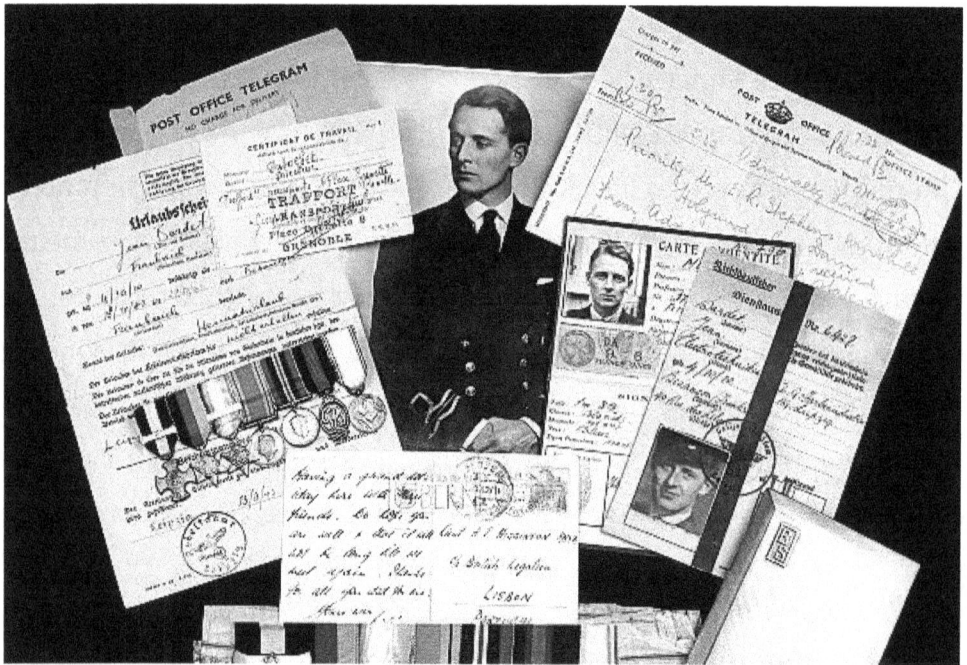

Lieutenant Commander William "Billie" Stephens forged documents

William (Billie) Stephens was the son of a Belfast shipping agent and timber importer. He was born in Belfast and educated at Shrewsbury before joining his father's firm. He joined the Royal Naval Volunteer Reserve in 1930 and at the outbreak of the Second World War joined the coastal forces

He received a commission to command a Motor Launch; this was a relatively small vessel measuring one hundred and twelve feet, weighing eighty-five tons and was capable of speeds up to twenty knots.

Motor Launch 192

Billie was heavily involved in what is now known as a famous raid on St Nazaire on the Burgundy coast on 27 March 1942. He commanded his Motor Launch 192 with considerable skill and bravery. Intelligence reports intimated that the new German battleship "Tirpitz" was now completed although in need of some last minute repairs. The size of the battleship meant the only dry dock available to her was at St Nazair on the mouth of the river Loire.

A plan was hatched, "Operation Chariot": a daring scheme whereby the destroyer Cambeltown packed with five tons of explosives would ram the gates of the dock blowing them up. Two destroyers escorted Cambletown on her mission and an armada of smaller vessels including sixteen motor launches. As Cambletown steamed full throttle towards the gates she came under extreme enemy fire however, unstoppable, she hit the lock gates at 1.30am.

The fast and manoeuvrable motor launches drew their fare share of fire, as was their mission. Only four of the sixteen returned to Britain.

Billie Stephens was in command of one of the leading motor launches they were almost abeam of the harbour wall when the launch was hit by intensive gunfire. Completely immobilised and on fire he had no option but to order his men to abandon ship. Managing to swim ashore carrying the wounded sailors they were taken prisoner by the Germans.

The Cambeltown eventually blew up destroying the main gate and killing a number of German officers.

Stephens and his crew were taken to a courtyard where they were searched and then lined up against a wall. The men knew their destiny. Fortunately, an officer arrived and took control ensuring the safety of the prisoners. The British officers and sailors were imprisoned in an underground store without food or water despite having several wounded men. The prisoners were then transported to Stalag 133 where they endured appalling conditions. Stephens was sent to Wilhelmshaven and interrogated at great length before being sent to Marlag from where he made his first escape. En route to Oflag IV C (Colditz) Billie jumped from the train, he was captured the next day and sent on to Colditz to serve a week in solitary confinement.

Major Pat Reid, in The Colditz Story (1952) recalled his early impression of Stephens:

> *'He was handsome, fair-haired, with piercing blue eyes and Nelsonian nose. He walked as if he was permanently on the deck of a ship. He was a daredevil, and his main aim appeared to be to force his way into the German area of the camp and then hack his way out with a metaphorical cutlass.'*

Five weeks later, Stephens and Major Ronnie Littledale submitted their plan to the escape committee. It was accepted. They requested two other POWs to join them one was to have lock-picking skills. Hank Wardle was chosen for this task, along with Major Reid as the second member.

They began their extensive preparation over the following days using the experiences of other successful escapes.

Reid insisted that each man carry a small suitcase to give them all a look of respectability, he thought travelling without one would signal they were fugitives.

Wearing balaclavas and socks over their shoes with their suitcases under their arms filled with sheets they began their escape.

On 14th October wearing balaclavas, gloves and socks over their shoes and carrying their suitcases muffled with blankets containing sheets, they began their escape Pat Reid led the way through a kitchen window. Once in position Reid was able to signal back to the others when the coast was clear they could then proceed through the window. The next stage was barred window, which gave them access to a flat roof well illuminated: a guard was only fifteen yards away.

The Battle of Britain pilot, Douglas Bader, was acting as an observer conducting the "Colditz Orchestra". The plan involved the orchestra pausing when a guard had his back to them. This enabled each of the four men to make a dash for the shadows of a ventilator safely. The critical next hurdle of the escape was a narrow flue. Stripping naked they managed to squeeze through. Somewhat battered and bruised they dressed in a nearby shrubbery. Strolling nonchalantly past the sleeping sentry in the barracks they continued on. Knotting the sheets they dropped in three stages, fifty-four feet in total into a dry moat.

Billie started to cough when he reached the ground bring attention to himself and the others. He quickly stuffed his mouth full of grass and dirt in an act of desperation.

The men then climbed the outer wall, which was only ten feet high. At 4am they shook hands split into two pairs and Stephens and Littledale set off together.

They strolled to a station at Rochlitz trying not to bring attention to themselves. Catching the train to Chemnitz en route to Nuremberg they changed at Hoff, where they sat in the station drinking beer. The escapees had been warned to keep away from Stuttgart; it was far too dangerous. Travelling on minor rail lines they eventually reached Tubingen. After two days of trekking they reached the Swiss border crossing under the cover of darkness. Their journey from Colditz had taken only five days. Reid and Wardle had travelled a different route arriving the day before. All were interned in Switzerland.

The Swiss released the group after questioning, Stephens made his way to France continuing on over the Pyrenees and into Spain The Spanish authorities arrested him and once again Billie found himself in prison. Billie was a charmer, he bribed a guard with his wristwatch to allow him to telephone the British Embassy in Madrid. The British smuggled him out in the boot of a Cadillac to Gibraltar and from there he flew to the UK.

After the war Stephens returned to Northern Ireland to continue with the family business. He became chairman of Northern Bank and the Northern Ireland Tourist Board as well as Commissioner of Belfast Harbour and High Sheriff of County Down. He was also involved in the Missions to Seamen.

This debonair man, full of charisma, was always immaculate, fit and alert. He had a certain magic and an excitement to him. He was absolutely devoted to his Swiss wife Chou-chou who sheltered him after he crossed the Swiss border. They delighted in entertaining their many friends and in playing endless hours of bridge and the French edition of Scrabble. In the late Eighties they moved to France, to a cottage near Nice for the sake of her health. Her death in 1993 was a severe blow to him.

Prisoners made many attempts to escape Oflag IV-C (Colditz). Approximately thirty-six men succeeded in their attempts.

The German Army made Colditz a Sonderlager (high-security prison camp), the only one of its type located within Germany. Field Marshal Hermann Göring declared Colditz "escape-proof" yet despite this audacious claim, there were multiple escapes by British, Australian, Canadian, French, Polish, Dutch, and Belgian inmates. Despite some misapprehensions to the contrary, Colditz Castle was not used as a Prisoner-of-War camp in World War I.

Prisoners were inventive in devising methods to escape. They duplicated keys to various doors, made copies of maps, forged Ausweise (identity papers), and manufactured their own tools. MI9, a department of the British War Office which specialized in escape equipment, communicated with the prisoners in code and smuggled them new escape aids disguised in care packages from family or from non-existent charities, although they never tampered with Red Cross care packages for fear it would force the Germans to stop their delivery to all camps. The Germans became skilled at intercepting packages containing contraband material.

Prisoners also used items from their Red Cross parcels to buy information and tools from guards and local villagers

If a P.O.W. was lucky enough to escape from Colditz they would then face the considerable challenge of negotiating their way to a neutral country.

Dutch naval lieutenant Hans Larive discovered "The Singen Route" into Switzerland in 1940. On his first escape attempt Larive was caught near Singen, close to the Swiss border. The interrogating Gestapo officer was so confident the war would soon be won by Germany that he told Larive the safe way across the border. Larive did not forget and many prisoners later escaped using this route.

Most of the attempted escapes failed. Pat Reid, a British officer, failed to escape at first but then was appointed as "Escape Officer" in charge of coordinating the various escape groups. The Escape Officer would ensure escapes were controlled and not tripping over each other's attempts. Escape Officers were generally not permitted to escape while they held that position.

Many POWs tried unsuccessfully to escape in disguise: Airey Neave, a British officer, twice dressed as a guard and attempted to simply walk out A French Lieutenant, Boulé disguised himself as a woman. British Lieutenant Michael Sinclair even dressed as the German Sergeant Major Rothenberger when he tried to organize a mass escape, and French Lieutenant Perodeau disguised as regular camp electrician Willi Pöhnert ("Little Willi"):

On the night of 28 December 1942, one of the French officers blew out the fuse on the lights in the courtyard. As they had anticipated Pöhnert was summoned, and while he was still fixing the lights, Lieutenant Perodeau, dressed almost identically to Pöhnert and carrying a tool box, walked casually out of the courtyard gate. He passed the first guard without incident, but the guard at the main gate asked for his token — tokens were issued to each guard and staff member upon entry of the camp guardhouse specifically to avoid this type of escape — with no hope of bluffing his way out of this, Perodeau surrendered.

Dutch sculptors made two clay heads to stand in for escaping officers in the roll call. Later, "ghosts", officers who had faked a successful escape and hid in the castle, took the place of escaping prisoners in the roll call in order to delay discovery as long as possible.

Camp guards collected so much escape equipment that they established a "Commandant's Escape Museum". Local photographer Johannes Lange took photographs of the would-be escapers in their disguises or re-enacting their attempts for the camera. Along with the Lange photographs, one of the two sculpted clay heads was displayed proudly in the museum.

There was only one confirmed fatality during the escape attempts: British Lieutenant Michael Sinclair in September 1944. Sinclair attempted a repeat of the 1941 French over the wire escape. Security officer Eggers warned him after which Sinclair was fired upon by guards. A bullet hit Sinclair on the elbow and ricocheted through his heart.

The Germans buried him in Colditz cemetery with full military honours — his casket was draped with a Union Jack flag made by the German guards, and he received a seven-gun salute. Post-war he was awarded the Distinguished Service Order, the only man to receive it for escaping during World War II. He is currently buried in grave number 10.1.14 at Berlin War Cemetery in the Charlottenburg-Wilmersdorf district of Berlin.

Flight Lieutenant Dominic Bruce was a tiny-framed individual. He arrived at Colditz in 1942 after attempting to escape from Spangenberg Castle disguised as a Red Cross doctor. A new Commandant arrived at Colditz in the summer of 1942; he enforced rules restricting prisoners' personal belongings. On 8 September POWs were told to pack up all excess belongings and an assortment of boxes were delivered to carry them into store. Dominic Bruce immediately seized his chance and was packed inside a Red Cross packing case, three-foot square, with just a file and a forty foot length rope made of bed sheets. Bruce was taken to a storeroom on the third floor of the German Kommandantur and made his escape that night. When the German guards discovered the bed rope dangling from the window the following morning they raced to the storeroom and found the empty box. Bruce had inscribed 'Die Luft in Colditz gefällt mir nicht mehr. Auf Wiedersehen'! — "The air in Colditz no longer agrees with me. See you later!"

Bruce was recaptured a week later trying to stow aboard a Swedish ship in Danzig.

Bruce's Escape Box

In late 1940, British officer Peter Allan found out that the Germans were moving several mattresses from the castle to another camp and decided that would be his way out. He let the French officers moving the mattresses know that one would be a little bit heavier. Allan, a fluent German speaker, dressed himself up in a Hitlerjugend (Hitler Youth) uniform, stuffed Reichsmark in his pockets, and had himself sewn into one of the mattresses. He managed to get himself loaded into the truck, and unloaded into an empty house within the town.

Cutting himself out of the mattress several hours later when there was complete silence he climbed out of the window and into the garden and swaggered down the road towards his freedom.

Making his way to Vienna one hundred and sixty kilometres down the road via Stuttgart he got a lift with a senior SS officer. Allan recalled that ride as the scariest moment of his life. He had been aiming to reach Poland but soon after reaching Vienna found his money had run out. America had not yet entered the war so Allan decided to ask the American consulate for assistance; he was refused. His stepmother, Lois Allan, was a U.S. citizen he was sure the embassy would take him in. Allan had been on the run at this point for nine days; broke, exhausted, and hungry, he fell asleep in a park. Upon waking he discovered he was too weak to walk. Soon after he was picked up and returned to Colditz, where he spent the next three months in solitary confinement.

On 12 May 1941, Polish Lieutenants Miki Surmanowicz and Mietek Chmiel attempted to rappel down a thirty-six meter wall to freedom on a rope constructed out of bed sheets. In order to get into a suitable position both men orchestrated punishment in solitary confinement. After forcing open the door and picking the locks they made their way to the courtyard where they climbed up to a narrow ledge. From the ledge they were able to cross to the guardhouse roof, and climb through an open window on the outer wall. Utilising their bed sheet rope, they lowered themselves towards the ground. Both were caught when the German guards heard the hobnailed boots of one of the escapees scraping down the outside of the guardhouse wall. The guard who spotted the escapees shouted 'Hände hoch!!' [Hands up!!] to the men as they were descending the rope. As if.

The French lady

On June 5 1941, while returning from the park to the castle, some British prisoners noticed that a passing lady dropped her watch. One of the British POWs called out to her, but the lady just kept walking. This aroused the suspicion of the German guards and, upon inspection, "she" was revealed to be a French officer – Lieutenant Chasseurs Alpins Bouley.

The Canteen Tunnel

Early in 1941, the British prisoners had gained access to the sewers and drains which ran beneath the floors of the castle. Entrance to these was from a manhole cover in the floor of the canteen. After initial reconnaissance trips it was decided that the drain should be extended and an exit made in a small grassy area, which was overlooked from the canteen window. From there they planned to climb down the hill and drop below the steep outside eastern wall of the castle. The escapees knew which sentry would be on duty during the night of the escape, they pooled their resources and collected 500 Reichsmark for a bribe. This plan took three months to prepare. On the evening of 29 May 1941, Pat Reid hid in the canteen after it had been locked up for the night. Having removed the bolt from the lock on the door, he returned to the courtyard. After evening roll call the escapers slipped into the canteen unnoticed. They entered the tunnel and waited for the signal to proceed. Unknown to the prisoners, they had been betrayed by the bribed guard. Waiting on the grassy area to greet them was Hauptmann Priem, the commandant and his guard force.

Pat Reid recalls:

"I climbed out on to the grass and Rupert Barry was following close behind. My shadow was cast on the wall of the Kommandantur, and at that moment I noticed a second shadow beside my own. It held a gun. I yelled to Rupert to get back as a voice behind me shouted, Hände hoch! Hände hoch!. I turned to face a German officer levelling his pistol at me."

Behind him were seven British and four Polish officers. On his order the remaining men backed up the tunnel to evade detection but the Germans were waiting for them outside the canteen. Not wanting to give their captors any satisfaction the British burst into laughter as they came out.

Hauptmann Priem ends the story:

"And the Guard? He kept his 100 Marks; he got extra leave, promotion and the War Service Cross."

The French Tunnel

Nine French officers organised a long-term tunnel-digging project, the longest attempted out of Colditz Castle throughout the war. Deciding that the exit should be on the steep drop leading down towards the recreation area, outside the eastern walls of the castle. The officers began to scout for a possible location for the entrance. Lieutenants Cazaumayo and Paille had previously gained access to the clock tower in 1940. Both officers knew how to solve the problem.

Their tunnel began at the top of the chapel's clock tower and descended nearly nine meters into the ground using the shaft containing the ropes and weights for the clock. They discovered the weights and chains had been removed. This left an empty shaft, which extended from the clock to the cellars below. After the 1940 escape attempt by Cazaumayo and Paille the doors, which provided access to the tower, had been bricked up in order to prevent further attempts. However, by sealing up the tower the Germans had in essence provided a secure location. Now work could be done without being noticed. The French gained access to the tower from the attic and descended thirty-five meters to the cellars. Work began on a horizontal shaft in June 1941. This shaft work would continue for a further eight months.

The horizontal shaft towards the chapel progressed four meters before they hit rock the decision was taken to dig upwards towards the chapel floor. From here the tunnel continued underneath the wooden floor of the chapel for a distance of thirteen and a half meters. For this to be achieved, seven heavy oak timbers in the floor had to be cut through. Homemade saws assembled from table knives were employed for this task. Once completed, the tunnel dropped vertically from the far corner of the chapel a further five meters. The tunnel then proceeded out towards the proposed exit with two further descents separated by shafts in the stone foundations of the castle. The tunnel now ran a horizontal distance of forty-four meters reaching a final depth of eight and a half meters below the surface.

Tunnelling continued well into 1942. By then Germans knew that the French were digging somewhere, based on the noise of their digging reverberating through the castle at night. The French thought the tunnel's entrance was undetectable. However, on 15 January the Germans eventually searched the clock tower. Noise was heard below, and after lowering a small boy down the shaft three French officers were found. After searching the cellar thoroughly the entrance to the tunnel was eventually discovered a mere two meters short of completion. The French officers were convinced they had been betrayed by one of their own countrymen but this was never proven.

The tunnel had electric lighting along its whole length, powered by electricity from the chapel. Five large stones covering a small door, which left little trace of any hole, concealed the entrance to the tunnel in the wine cellar

The "Colditz Cock" glider

One of the most ambitious and imaginative escape attempts from Colditz was the idea of building a glider and flying to freedom. The idea came from two British pilots, Jack Best and Bill Goldfinch. Two army officers, Tony Rolt and David Walker who had recently arrived in the camp, encouraged them. It would be Tony Rolt who would recommend the chapel roof; he noticed it was obscured from the view of the Germans.

The two-man glider was to be assembled by the two pilots in the lower attic above the chapel it was to be launched from the roof to give it the elevation to fly across the river Mulde which was about sixty meters below. The runway was constructed from tables and the glider was to be launched using a pulley system based on a falling metal bathtub full of concrete, which would accelerate the glider to fifty kilometres an hour.

Prisoners built a false wall to hide the space in the attic where they slowly built the glider out of stolen wood. The Germans were incensed on discovering tunnels not secret workshops therefore the prisoners felt safe from detection. However, they still placed lookouts and created an electric alarm system to warn the builders of approaching guards.

Hundreds of ribs for the fuselage had to be constructed; they smuggled in timber predominantly from bed slats but also from every other piece of wood the POW's could obtain. The wing spars were constructed from floorboards. Control wires were made from electrical wiring taken from unused portions of the castle. A glider expert, Lorne Welch, reviewed the stress diagrams and calculations made by Goldfinch.

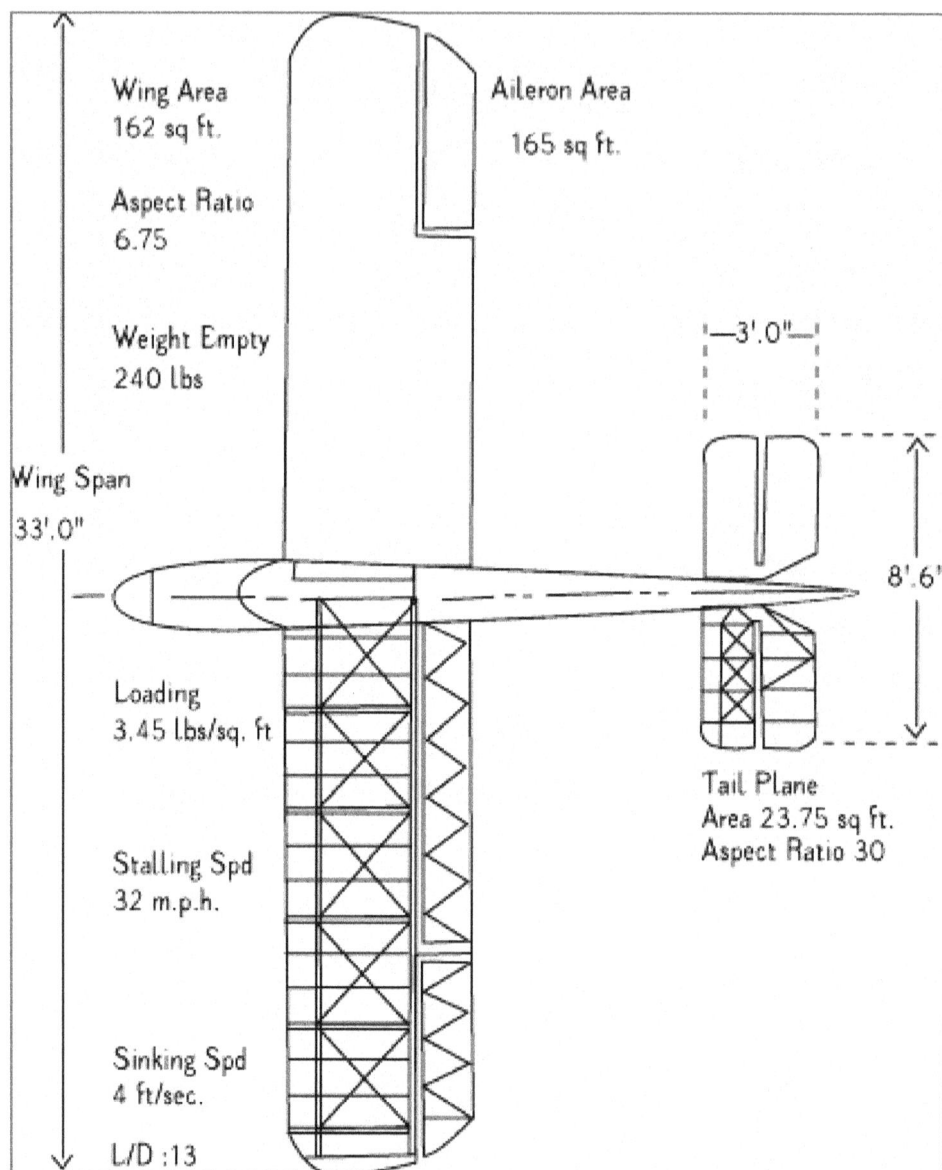

Wing Area
162 sq ft.

Aspect Ratio
6.75

Weight Empty
240 lbs

Aileron Area
165 sq ft.

—3'.0"—

Wing Span
33'.0"

Loading
3.45 lbs/sq. ft

Stalling Spd
32 m.p.h.

Sinking Spd
4 ft/sec.

L/D :13

8'.6"

Tail Plane
Area 23.75 sq ft.
Aspect Ratio 30

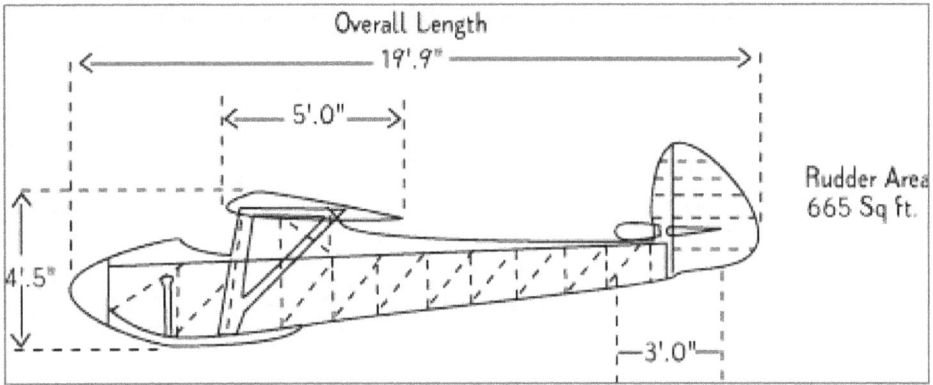

Overall Length 19'.9"
5'.0"
4'.5"
3'.0"
Rudder Area 665 Sq ft.

The resulting glider was to be a one hundred and nine kilograms two-seater, high wing, monoplane design. It had a Mooney style rudder and square elevators. The wingspan was thirty-three feet and the fuselage length was nineteen feet. Prison sleeping bags of blue and white checked cotton were used to provide the skin for the glider. German ration millet was boiled and used to seal the cloth pores.

The war ended before the glider was finished.

It was flown for a film on Colditz and it was a successful flight.

Tools Created for the Construction

Side-framed saw

handle of beech bed board

frame of iron window bars

blade of gramophone spring with 8 teeth / in (3 mm teeth)

Minute saw for fine work

gramophone spring blade, 25 teeth / in (1 mm teeth)

5/8 in (16 mm) metal drill obtained by bribery

Drill bits for making holes made from nails

A gauge made of beech, with cupboard bolt and gramophone needle

Large plane, 14½ in (368 mm) long

Home Made Plane

2 inch blade obtained by bribing a German guard

Wooden box (four pieces of beech screwed together)

Small plane, 8½ in (216 mm) long blade made from a table knife

Plane, 5 in (127 mm) long

Square made of beech with gramophone spring blade

Set of keys including:

Universal door pick, forged from a bucket handle

Successful Escape attempts

It is claimed that there were thirty-six "home runs" i.e. successful escapes from Colditz.

At the end of May 1943, the Armed Forces High Command decided that Colditz should hold only British and Commonwealth officers As a result all of the Dutch and Polish prisoners and most of the French and Belgians were moved to other camps in July. Three British officers tried their luck by impersonating French officers when they were moved out but they were later returned to Colditz. German security gradually improved and by the end of 1943 most of the potential avenues of escape had been eliminated. Several officers tried to escape during transit without success.

Some officers faked illnesses including mental illness in order to be repatriated on medical grounds. A member of the Royal Army Medical Corps (RAMC), Captain Ion Ferguson wrote a letter to an Irish friend suggesting Ireland join the war; the censors stopped the letter but his wish to be moved elsewhere was granted.. Four other British officers claimed symptoms of stomach ulcer, insanity, high blood pressure and back injury in order to be repatriated. However, there were also officers who went genuinely insane.

French Lieutenant Alain Le Ray escaped April 11, 1941. He hid in a terrace house in a park during a game of football. He was the first successful Colditz escaper and the first to reach neutral Switzerland.

French Lieutenant René Collin escaped May 31, 1941. He climbed into the rafters of a pavilion during exercise hiding there until dark he slipped away. He made it back to France.

French Lieutenant Pierre Mairesse Lebrun escaped July 2, 1941. He was captured. At a later date he vaulted over a wire fence in a park with the help of an associate. He reached Switzerland in eight days on a stolen bicycle.

Dutch Lieutenant Hans Larive escaped August 15, 1941. He hid under a manhole cover in the exercise enclosure emerging after nightfall Hans took a train to Gottmadingen reaching Switzerland in three days.

British Lieutenant Airey M. S. Neave escaped January 5, 1942. He crawled through a hole in a camp theatre to a guardhouse and marched out dressed as a German soldier. reaching Switzerland two days later.

Dutch Lieutenant Anthony Luteyn escaped January 5, 1942 with Neave.

British Lieutenant Hedley Fowler escaped September 9, 1942. Slipped out with four others through a guard office and a storeroom dressed as German officers and Polish orderlies. Only he and Van Doorninck reached Switzerland. Like Luteyn and Neave, this was another successful British Dutch effort.

Dutch Lieutenant Damiaen Joan van Doorninck escaped September 9, 1942 with Fowler.

British Capt. Patrick R. Reid escaped October 14, 1942. He slipped through the kitchen into the German yard then into the

Kommandantur cellar and down to a dry moat through the park. He took four days to reach Switzerland.

Canadian Flight Lieutenant Howard D. Wardle (RAF) escaped October 14, 1942 with Reid.

British Major Ronald B. Littledale escaped October 14, 1942 with Reid.

British Lieutenant-Commander William E. Stephens escaped October 14, 1942 with Littledale.

British Lieutenant William A. Millar escaped January, 1944. He broke into a German courtyard and hid in a truck intending to go to Czechoslovakia. He never reached home and is listed missing on the Bayeux memorial. There is speculation that he was caught and executed in Mauthausen concentration camp as a victim of the secret Kugel-erlass (Bullet Decree) July 15, 1944.

French Lieutenants J. Durand-Hornus, G. de Frondeville and J. Prot escaped while on a visit to the town dentist December 17, 1941.

Polish Lieutenant Kroner was transferred to Königswartha Hospital where he jumped out of the window.

French Lieutenant Boucheron fled from Zeitz Hospital, was recaptured, and later escaped from Düsseldorf prison.

French Lieutenants Odry and Navelet escaped from Elsterhorst Hospital.

British Captain Louis Rémy escaped from Gnaschwitz military hospital. His three companions were captured, but he reached Algeciras by boat, and later Britain.

British Squadron Leader Brian Paddon escaped to Sweden via Danzig

French Lieutenant Raymond Bouillez escaped from a hospital after an unsuccessful attempt to jump from a train.

Dutch Lieutenant J. van Lynden slipped away when the Dutch were moved to Stanislau camp.

French Lieutenant A. Darthenay escaped from a hospital at Hohenstein-Ernstthal, later joined the French Resistance, and was killed by the Gestapo on April 7, 1944.

Indian RAMC Captain Birendra Nath Mazumdar M.D. was the only Indian in Colditz. He went on a hunger strike to have himself transferred into an Indian-only camp. His wish was granted three weeks later and he escaped from that camp to France and reached Switzerland in 1944 with the aid of the French Resistance.

W. E. "Wally" Hammond (from the sunken submarine HMS Shark) and Don "Tubby" Lister (from the captured submarine HMS Seal) campaigned for a transfer from Colditz, arguing that he was not an officer. He was transferred to Lamsdorf prison escaped from a Breslau work party and reached England via Switzerland in 1943.

Colditz was not the prison Goring described as 'escape proof' the officers from the allied countries showed initiative, courage and invention to prove him wrong.

The Aussie Larrikin

Why Hitler Had Willy Shot

Chapter 16

Willy Williams

Squadron Leader John "Willy" Williams was a boy from Manly, Sydney, Australia. Willy became a World War II ace and briefly, one of the youngest squadron leaders in the history of the RAF. The average life expectancy of an RAF pilot was rather short so senior pilots tended to be young.

Willy in the Middle East

Willy survived being shot down over France and ended up as a POW in Stalag Luft III on the German-Polish border. This was a camp purpose built to be escape proof. The commandant, Luftwaffe Colonel von Luger, told the senior British officer, Group Captain Ramsey.

'There will be no escapes from this camp.'

'It is our duty to try to escape.' replied Ramsey.

Willy would become an integral player in what became known as "The Great Escape".

The men demonstrated ingenuity along with great organization skills and mental toughness to achieve the ultimate escape. Seventy-six prisoners tunnelled out of the so-called "escape proof" camp right under the German's noses.

Willy played a major role in planning and excavating the tunnels. He did make it through the tunnel along with his good schoolmate Reginald "Rusty" Keirath.

They were both heading for Switzerland along the German Czech border when they were captured.

Hitler was so infuriated that so many had escaped he ordered the summary execution of fifty officers. Willy and Rusty died together in a dark forest at the hand of a Gestapo officer and a Luger pistol.

At the Nuremberg trials after the war twenty Gestapo officers were sentenced to hang for this atrocity.

The Great Escape

If you were unfortunate enough to be captured by the Germans in World Two you could do a lot worse than been sent to Stalag Luft 111 (Sagan). The housing and recreational facilities were better than most prisoner of war camps.

A Barracks at Stalag Luft 111

British and American airmen were the predominant inmates they had mostly been shot down over Axis territory.

However, it was the sworn duty of all captured military personnel to continue to fight the enemy by surviving, communicating information and escaping. Many of the prisoners at Sagan were re-captured escapees. The Germans believed that security at the new camp would make it impossible to escape.

Many of the POWs were officers with strong organisational skills; they knew if any escape was to be successful it had to be well planned.

The prisoners at Sagan therefore established an "escape committee". The chief escape officer was Squadron Leader Roger Bushell, a former escapee who had been recaptured several times. He was known as 'Big X'.

It was decided to build three tunnels and free two hundred POWs. The tunnels were given the names of "Tom" "Dick" and "Harry".

The problem they needed to resolve was twofold, how to dispose of the dirt from the dig and how to support the tunnel to prevent it from collapsing.

Bed boards were used just as they were at Colditz; the same problem of no support for their mattresses also occurred in both camps; some rigged up hammocks.

Bed Boards in the Tunnel

A major problem was how to dispose of the soil from the tunnel; the colour of the soil was different from what surrounded their barracks and the camp overall.

One method they used was to manufacture long bags which could be filled with earth then hidden in the prisoner's trouser legs. A cord around the neck would open the bags thus releasing the earth on a patch of ground that was being dug or cultivated by another prisoner. Those dispersing the dirt in this way were known as "Penguins". More than one hundred tons of earth was disposed of in this way. Another method involved filling empty Red Cross boxes, placing the boxes in the middle of a group of men who would then gradually bury the earth.

An integral group within the escape group were the forgers; they were responsible for creating maps and identity papers.

Tailors were also critical to the escapee's success, they made civilian clothes out of blankets and other materials that were scrounged and altered uniforms.

The German guards discovered "Tom". This was a major blow to the success of the escape. The escape committee decided to suspend all digging in "Dick" and "Harry" until they felt safe to recommence activities.

When things settled down they were able to complete "Harry" the great escape was planned for 24th March 1944. It was a perfect moonless night to depart Sagan and the Germans hospitality!

The committee decided the only fair way to decide who went and who stayed was to draw lots.

On the fateful night the escapees congregated in hut 104, the plan was to leave the camp in stages.

One prisoner was appointed to breakout of the tunnel to ensure the exit came in the woods out of sight of the guards. He returned with disturbing news; the tunnel was about ten feet short of the woods. This would mean they were directly in the path of the guard patrolling the perimeter fence. The committees hastily met and devised a methodology, which would indicate to the man coming up through the tunnel exit that he could proceed.

Time was their enemy and it was now past 10pm, a decision was made that the escape would cease at 5am. It was also very clear with the time available that the two hundred man target would not be met.

At 4.45am they heard rifle shots, the tunnel exit had been discovered.

Seventy Six men had escaped through the tunnel. Those that were found waiting their turn in hut 104 were sent to the solitary confinement cells.

Of the seventy-six men who escaped, three made it home to the UK. Twenty Three were recaptured and sent back to Sagan. Hitler personally ordered the execution of the other fifty men including Willy and Rusty.

The commandant of Stalag Luft III, Lindeiner, was court-martialled by the Gestapo for not preventing the escape.

Love Conquers the Wall

Chapter 17

Horace Greasly

Horace Greasley was born on Christmas Day in 1918 along with twin brother Harold, to Joseph and Mabel Greasley. The Greasley twins grew up in the village of Ibstock, where they worked on their family's farm.

Horace and Harold were inseparable and both boys were popular with the girls of the village not only for their good looks but their bravado bordering on larrikinism.

Both enjoyed working on the family farm where they kept dairy cattle and pigs. In both their minds living on a farm for the rest of their lives would suit them down to the ground.

Circumstances changed, the farm could not sustain them all so Horace left the farm to become a hairdresser. He was cutting the mayors hair when news came in that Hitler's army had invaded Czechoslovakia. He knew immediately that he would be liable to be called up along with Harold.

They were both conscripted in the first draft.

Soon after his call up notification was received a regular client offered to get him a job as a fireman, a reserved occupation which would actually pay better than joining the services and would keep him out of the firing line. Horace turned the offer down.

Both twins trained with the 2nd/5th Battalion Leicestershire Regiment and were dispatched off to France as part of the British Expeditionary Force.

Horace and Harold had no idea what they were in for.

The German and Allied forces were roughly evenly matched. The Germans offensive fielded one hundred and thirty six divisions against ninety-four French divisions, and ten British divisions of the British

Expeditionary Force. Twenty-two Belgian and nine Dutch divisions completed the allied forces. The numbers of tanks fielded on each side was also approximately equal. It was only in the air that the Germans enjoyed massive superiority: two thousand five hundred aircraft against a few hundred British, and largely obsolete French aircraft.

The quantity of the Allied troops was fine; the quality was not. Britain and France had been largely unprepared for war, and the training of their conscript armies was abysmal. In Britain, ammunition shortages meant each recruit was allowed only five rounds in total for rifle training. The French conscripts were even less trained. Fortunately, the small British Expeditionary Force had many professional troops to reinforce the recent conscripts.

By contrast the Germans had had much more intensive and elaborate training. Hitler knew there would be a war! Accurate, full-scale mock-ups of crucial fortifications were built in Germany, and troops rehearsed their attacks until perfect.

The Allies were defeated, the High Command knew they had to evacuate

over three hundred and fifty thousand men including the British French and Belgian divisions who were trapped in the port of Dunkirk. The British decided to evacuate them by sea. Initially, they believed that they would be able to rescue, about thirty thousand men. Over the course of ten incredible days from May 26 to June 4, they accomplished a magnificent feat. The navy put out a call for help from the civilian population and boats from all over Britain began appearing

Fishing boats, yachts, pleasure boats, rowboats, all answered the call. Under constant aerial attack the navy and civilians evacuated nearly Three hundred and forty thousand men. They had to leave behind all of their heavy equipment but that could be replaced. When it was over, Britain still had an army with which to fight another day.

For every seven soldiers who escaped through Dunkirk, one man was left behind as a prisoner of war (POW). The majority of these prisoners were sent on forced marches into Germany. Horace was one of those captured.

What followed was a ten week forced march across France and Belgium to Holland and a three-day train journey to prison camps in Polish Silesia, then annexed as part of Germany. Many died on the way, Greasley reckoned himself lucky to have survived.

In the second POW camp to which he was assigned, near Lamsdorf, he encountered the seventeen year-old daughter of the director of the marble quarry to which the camp was attached.

She was working, as an interpreter for the Germans There was a mutual attraction between Horace and this beautiful young girl.

Within a few weeks Horace and Rosa were having an intimate relationship right under the German's noses. They would meet in all sorts of hiding places including the camp work sheds; nothing would dampen their lust for each other. Unfortunately after one year of their relationship Horace was transferred to Freiwaldau, an annex of Auschwitz, some forty miles away.

Rosa

There was only one way to continue their lustful relationship, break out of his new camp. Security at Freiwaldau was not very tight as it was located on the border of Germany and Polish Silesia; there was little hope of escaping back to Britain. The nearest neutral country was Sweden, four hundred and twenty miles to the north.

Greasley reasoned that short absences could be disguised or go unnoticed. Messages were exchanged between him and Rosa via members of village work parties and handed to Horace, the camp barber, when they had their hair cut.

Horace, with the help of mates, would go under the wire to meet Rosa, they made wild passionate love and he would break back into the camp under the cover of darkness.

Greasley recalled that in some weeks he made the return journey three or more times depending on whether Rosa's translation duties brought her close to his camp. His proven bravado to continue their love affair was not the only testimony to his daring. This photograph shows Heinrich Himmler, head of the SS, inspecting a prison camp and a shirtless skinny POW close to the fence confronting him.

Horace Confronts Himmler

The prisoner was Horace Greasley; he is shown with his shirt off demonstrating to Himmler that they were not being fed enough and that all the POW's were as thin as he was.

Horace had no idea who Himmler was but survived the introduction. The food rations were not increased.

Rosa did help with his nutrition by giving him food parcels to take back to the camp, she also smuggled radio parts, which enabled the prisoners to keep up with the news by listening to the BBC.

Horace broke out of camp two hundred times. He broke back in two hundred times. This made Horace Grimsley the greatest escapologist in history!

Horace was held in captivity for five years, he was finally liberated on 24 May 1945, he returned to Britain and continued the relationship with Rosa via letters soon after the war, he even provided her with a reference allowing her to work as a translator for the Americans.

Sometime after Horace returned home he received the very sad news that Rosa had died during childbirth, the newborn died as well. Although Rosa never told him of her pregnancy, he knew in his heart of hearts that the child was his. Horace was heartbroken.

The love affair conducted with Rosa was a dangerous one not only because of the constant danger of the escapes but unknown to Horace she was Jewish. If the authorities had discovered her ancestry both would have been hanged.

Horace and Rosa proved the adage "Love Conquers All"

The One that Got Away

Chapter 18

Franz von Werra

Franz von Werra was born to upper class Swiss parents who were in fact paupers. So poor that they decided to sell both he and his sister to an aristocratic German family.

Both children attended excellent schools and were brought up as well-bred German children. At the age of eighteen Franz joined the

Luftwaffe. Regarded by some as arrogant others regarded him as personable and highly intelligent. One officer recalled Franz as 'an honest and pleasant young man; a bit of a showman with a wonderful imagination, but a reliable and honest chap.'

Battle of Britain was at its height in September 1940; Franz von Werra was flying his Me109 over England close to Love's Farm in Kent. Workers on the farm attending their crops heard a burst of gunfire from the nearby anti-aircraft battery. They looked up only to see a German fighter came into view flying low over the farm. The planes wheels were not extended, it was obvious the fighter was about to make a crash landing in a field a quarter of a mile away. This was how Franz von Werra came to Britain. He was soon placed under arrest and taken to Headquarters, Kent County Constabulary, in Maidstone. That evening, von Werra was handed over to the Army, who escorted him to Maidstone Barracks. In the morning an officer and two armed guards arrived and transported him to the London District Prisoner of War Cage. He was interrogated until the late afternoon then ordered back into the truck and taken to Cockfosters in London where he was questioned for the next two weeks.

Von Werra was transferred to a Prisoner of War camp, Grizedale Hall in the Lake District, Cumbria.

Franz knew that it would only be a matter of time before Germany invaded Britain but he was still determined to escape.

After about ten days in the camp Franz approached the "escape committee" with a plan for his escape, the plan was approved.

Part of the camp's daily routine was to take the prisoners outside through the village of Satterthwaite and beyond. Along the way was High Bowkerstead corner, where the party was always brought to a halt. Von Werra's plan was simply to make a run for it at that corner whilst a subtle diversion taking place to distract the attention of the guards.

At 2pm on Monday 7th October, von Werra and twenty-three of his fellow officers departed the camp for their walk. Their escort consisted ten armed guards including one officer. An officer being present was unusual, the supervision was normally left to two NCO's; one of whom was mounted on a horse. All decisions relating to the walk were therefore left to the mounted NCO. The senior POW, Lieutenant Colonel Hauptmann Pohle, sensed that the presence of the officer might create a little confusion to the accepted command structure. As the party drew near to the gate, Pohle called ahead to the NCO to lead the men southwards towards Satterthwaite. The NCO thinking that the order had come from his own officer, naturally obeyed.

The country roads around this area were usually deserted the odd motorcar or bicycle might come by occasionally but not very often.

The POW party arrived at High Bowkerstead corner only to find to their amazement a horse and cart approaching. The group stopped to let the old greengrocer pass by at a very slow pace. They had arrived at the stone wall where von Werra was planning to make his escape. The original plan was for one of the prisoners to approach the horse and give it a pat but as he moved forward to do so he was ordered back into line. Von Werner quickly changed his plan and when the horse and cart eventually passed the group he quickly climbed the wall and rolled over into the field. He departed unnoticed as his fell prisoners formed a human shield in front of the wall to hide him. The guards had no idea what had happened.

The Cumbrian landscape is amongst the most difficult terrains in England and it was unseasonably wet and cold for October. All over Cumbria were located hoggarths; small buildings made of stone used for farmyard storage.

When the guards realised that von Werra had escaped they notified the local farmers to keep a look out for him particularly in their hoggarths, as they knew the escapee would seek warmth and shelter at some stage.

The Home Guard were given the task of inspecting the hoggarths on a nightly basis

On the night of the 10th October in pouring rain two members of the Home Guard, approached a hoggarth in the vicinity of Broughton Mills and noticed that its lock had been forced. A light was shone inside and there crouching in the far corner was freshly shaven though gaunt von Werra. The home guard placed him under arrest and led down the hill. His hands were tied behind his back with cord held on tightly by one of the guards. As they reached the road at the bottom of the hill von Werra dragged his arms to the right pulling the guard off balance. Freeing his right arm he hit out at the guard knocking him to the ground. Wrenching his arms apart, von Werra's restraints came loose and he ran back up the hill and into woodland. The two old guards pursued him but had no chance of catching him, they gave up and returned home quite dejected.

At dawn police and soldiers sealed off the area and began combing the country side with the aid of blood hounds; they found no trace of the German escapee.

The search team gave up their pursuit and retired to the local pub for some well-earned refreshment. There was a shout coming from outside 'Tally ho' 'Tally ho' this was the call when a fox had been found. They raced outside to find old Joe Blakely who told them he spotted the German walking along the side of a wall about half a mile away.

By the time the search party had got to this position, von Werra had of course had disappeared. Surveying the scene one of the search team suddenly noticed some movement in the damp grass not twenty yards away. He ran to the spot and almost stood on top of von Werra who was lying on his back with his body submerged under the mud only his face was visible. He was handcuffed and returned to Grizedale Hall, where the Camp Commandant sentenced him to twenty-one days in solitary confinement. However, he did not complete this sentence. On 3rd November two days before he was due to be released he was informed that he was to be transferred to another camp.

Von Werra arrived at the Hayes Camp, in Swanwick, Derbyshire. Here he renewed his acquaintance with Major Fanelsa who had helped von Werra to escape from Grizedale Hall; he was now the Camp Leader at the Hayes. Franz allocated to the "Garden House" and soon involved himself with a group of would-be escapers. The group consisted of von Werra, his Austrian friend Lieutenant Wagner, Major Heinz Cramer, Lieutenant Walter Manhard and two other prisoners by the name of Willhelm and Malischewski. They called themselves "The Swanwick Construction Company." The objective of the company was to dig an escape tunnel.

In the north wing of the garden house they found a disused room, this is where they would start digging The tunnel was designed to be thirteen metres long and would pass beneath two security fences including the lane that lay between them. The exit emerged in a small patch of waste ground. There were a few trees and bushes offering some cover. The concept was presented to Major Fanelsa but he was not supportive. Despite his opposition the group started work on 17th November 1940.

The tunnelling team worked relentlessly particularly von Werra and his friend Walter Manhard. They achieved good progress through the clay soil however; it was difficult disposing the soil. They stored it in the roof space and even in the latrines but the sheer volume extracted from the dig meant they needed to find an alternative solution.

Fortunately, Manhard discovered a hole two feet in diameter beneath a stone slab at the front of the Garden House. Six feet beneath this they could see water. It turned out to be a large tank built for holding rainwater. This would be ideal for disposing the remainder of the soil. On 17th December 1940, the tunnel had been completed.

The employees of the Swanwick Construction Company prepared to depart. Forgers at the camp had provided the five escapers with props and papers whilst Willhelm had obtained some British money by selling a ring to one of the guards. At 8.15pm 20th December shortly after final roll call von Werra wearing a beret and pyjamas over the top of his flying suit made his way into the tunnel and began to work on creating the exit hole.

As anti-aircraft guns opened up on German bombers over Derby, the camp choir burst out into song even louder than usual. "Muss i den, muss i den, zum Stadteli hinaus" (I must away into the great wide world) was the song. Von Werra was suitably amused. Once out of the tunnel von Werra, Cramer, and Manhard had to lie low in the meadow next to the camp as civilians from the surrounding area were walking up and down the path. Once all was clear the five escapers went their separate ways with a pledge to meet up again in Berlin.

Manhard and Cramer stayed together. Their intention was to walk to Somercotes and then catch a bus to Nottingham. From there they planned to get to the East Coast. Unfortunately they lost their way and Cramer was captured. He was in the process of stealing a policeman's bicycle. Manhard proceeded alone catching a bus to Sheffield where he was captured. Willhelm and Wagner were found on the outskirts of Manchester hiding in the back of a lorry.

Von Werra remained alone having concocted a cavalier escape plan. He removed his pyjamas and was now in his flying suit. His intention was to pass himself off as a Dutch pilot serving with the RAF. This would allow him to enter an airbase and steal a plane. Whilst imprisoned in the camp he read as many English papers as possible, he felt comfortable with current events and was sure he could conduct a serious conversation with anyone he happened to meet while on his mission. Conscious of the fact that British bombers flew at night von Werra hid until 3am. Approaching a railway station he discovered a train sitting at the platform. He approached the driver and introduced himself as a member of the Royal Dutch Air Force serving with the RAF. Franz claimed he had been on a bombing raid that night and was shot down crash landing nearby. The driver agreed to help him get to the nearest RAF base.

Von Werra requested the use of a telephone to ring the RAF base so they could dispatch a car to pick him up and take him back to the airbase. He was informed he would have to wait until the booking clerk arrived at 6.00am, as he was the only one with a public phone. When Eaton, the booking clerk, arrived he was not happy with von Werra's story he decided to contact the police. Franz used his charm to convince Eaton of his authenticity and permitted him to call to RAF Hucknall, and arrange for a car to come and collect him. The police, however, arrived first. They questioned von Werra but again he was able to convince them that his story was true

The RAF staff car arrived and took Franz back to the base; so far his scheme was going to plan or so he thought.

Squadron Leader Boniface, the duty officer, greeted him that morning. Boniface was suspicious of von Werra's story and asked to see his identity disc. Von Werra was confident that the forged disc would pass muster however, when presented, it had faded badly. Von Werra made the excuse he needed to visit the toilet he took the opportunity to run back to the base entrance where he had seen hangers. He hoped to find a suitable plane to hijack. All the planes seemed to be waiting for major repairs none were suitable for his purposes. He climbed a security fence and found a number of Hurricanes, he approached a mechanic with the story that Wing Commander Boniface had ordered him to take the plane for a test flight.

The mechanic gave Franz a quick explanation of the controls and went to fetch the trolley-accumulator to start the engine.

While he was gone, Squadron Leader Boniface appeared alongside the aircraft with a revolver aimed at von Werra's head. That was to be end of this escape!

Von Werra received fourteen days in solitary confinement.

The British decided that all German POWs should be transported to Canada in January 1941.

Von Werner and another twelve hundred and fifty German prisoners set sail for Halifax, Nova Scotia. Franz did not stop fantasising about how he would escape from the ship but the reality was he landed in Halifax still a POW.

Loaded onto a train the prisoners were heading for a camp on the north shore of Lake Superior, Ontario.

Franz, yet again, decided he would attempt another escape. He figured the route they were taking would take them close to the border with the United States, which was still neutral at that point in time.

The plan was reasonably simple he would climb through the carriage's window and cross the border. The problem he had was the windows had iced over and with no tools it would be very difficult to remove it. He used his body warmth and others in the carriage also leant their warmth to defrost the ice. Eventually the window was clear.

Although they had managed to de-ice the window the space available would mean von Werra would have to squeeze through headfirst; a daunting prospect!

Franz readied himself as the train had just departed from a station and hadn't yet picked up full speed. A fellow prisoner got to his feet and held up a blanket as if he was folding it. Von Werner pushed himself out the window and landed in the snow unharmed. He found himself in Smiths Falls about thirty miles from the St Lawrence River, which formed the border with the United States.

It wasn't until the following afternoon that his absence noted by the guards.

He was able to obtain a map from a gas station and discovered his closest point to the St Lawrence was a town called Prescott, he walked two mile down river and decided to cross. The river had become ice. Halfway across he realised that the river was flowing there was no way he could make it across. He returned to the shore and found a dingy he dragged it the rivers edge and rowed across; he was now in neutral territory.

He immediately headed towards the town of Ogdensburg. He found a policeman and handed himself in. Von Werra convinced the police he was a German officer and a POW, they handed him over the immigration authorities. He was charged with entering the United States illegally and was in real fear of being handed back to the Canadians. He was permitted to contact the German Consul in New York and as a result received a significant amount of press. He became a celebrity recounting his exaggerated stories to all who would listen. While Franz was enjoying the good life in New York both Britain and Canada were negotiating for his return. In April 1941 the British and Canadians had negotiated von Werra's return. There was one small problem; von Werra was now in Berlin! He had escaped through Mexico then Brazil caught a ship to Barcelona then Rome and finally Berlin. All under the authorities noses!

Hitler awarded him the Iron Cross

Returning to military service, von Werra was posted to the Russian Front and then flew fighter patrols over the North Sea. On the 25th October 1941, von Werra was flying a routine patrol from Holland when his engine failed and his plane disappeared. No trace of either aircraft or pilot was ever found.

French Letters

Chapter 19

General Henri Giraud, a French Commander, was a celebrated warrior who had served in North Africa prior to World War One. He graduated from the Saint-Cyr Military Academy in 1900 and joined the French Army, commanding Zouave troops in North Africa until he was transferred back to France in 1914 when World War I broke out.

It was during World War One that Giraud was seriously wounded while serving as a captain. Giraud commanded a Battalion of Zouaves. In their day the Zouaves were better known than the French Foreign Legion, revered by their countrymen as tough, dashing, roistering daredevils -- the heroes of many a hard-fought battle, and the stuff of legend.

He was leading a bayonet charge during the Battle of Charleroi on 21 August 1914 when he was seriously wounded and left for dead on the battlefield. He was captured by the Germans and placed in a prison camp in Belgium. He managed to escape two months later by pretending to be a roustabout with a traveling circus. He then asked Edith Cavell for help, and eventually he was able to return to France via the Netherlands.

Edith Cavell was a British nurse. She is celebrated for saving the lives of soldiers from both sides without discrimination and in helping some two hundred Allied soldiers escape from German-occupied Belgium during the First World War, for which she was arrested. She was subsequently court-martialled, found guilty of treason and sentenced to death. Despite international pressure for mercy, she was shot by a German firing squad. Her execution received worldwide condemnation and extensive press coverage.

Once the end of the war was declared on the 11th November 1918 Giraud served with French troops in Constantinople under General Franchet d'Esperey. In 1933, he was transferred to Morocco to fight against Rif (kabyle) rebels. He was awarded the *Légion d'Honneur* after the capture of Abd-el-Krim and later became the military commander of Metz. He also taught military strategy at the École de Guerre, where one of his students was Captain Charles de Gaulle.

1940

When World War II began, Giraud became a member of the Superior War Council along with Charles de Gaulle, with whom he disagreed about the tactics of using armoured troops. He became the commander of the 7th Army when it was sent to the Netherlands on 10 May 1940 and was able to delay German troops at Breda on 13 May. As a consequence, many casualties occurred requiring the merger of the 7th Army with the 9th. Giraud was a General who led from the front; he was riding in a Jeep on a reconnaissance patrol when the Germans captured him; he had been trying to block a German attack through the Ardennes. A court-martial tried Giraud for ordering the execution of two German saboteurs wearing civilian clothes, but he was acquitted and taken to Königstein Castle near Dresden, which was used as a high-security POW prison.

Giraud planned his escape carefully over the following two years. He taught himself German and memorised a map of the surrounding area. He made a one hundred and fifty foot rope out of twine, torn bed sheets, and copper wire, which friends had smuggled, into the prison for him. Using a simple code embedded in his letters home, he informed his family of his plans to escape. On 17 April 1942, he lowered himself down the cliff of the mountain fortress. He had shaved off his moustache, and, donned a Tyrolean hat so he looked like a typical German local. Henri travelled to Schandau to meet his Special Operations Executive contact who provided him with a change of clothes, cash and identity papers. Through various ruses, he reached the Swiss border by train. To avoid border guards he trekked through the mountains until he was apprehended by two Swiss soldiers, who took him to Basle.

Giraud eventually made it into **Vichy France**, where he revealed his identity. He tried to convince **Marshal Pétain** that Germany could be beaten, and that France must resist the German occupation. His views were rejected, but the Vichy government refused to return Giraud to the Germans.

Safely in his beloved France, he was lauded by the French people for his escape, which gave them faith that the Germans would be ultimately defeated. Hitler was furious and ordered his capture and execution; he survived an assassination attempt in August 1944.

In November 1944 Giraud was taken by submarine from Gibraltar to meet with General Eisenhower to discuss his role in the Allied invasion. One condition he insisted on was that the French troops would support the American troops, not the British. He had a deep-seated mistrust of his cousins across the channel. He also demanded that he lead the invasion, a condition to which Eisenhower could not agree. Giraud eventually agreed to serve under Vichy Admiral Francois Darlan who had the support of both Eisenhower and Churchill. Darlan was assassinated on 24 December 1942, giving Giraud the opportunity to lead the French troops.

Giraud served as co-president of the French Committee of National Liberation with Charles de Gaulle. This was not a partnership that could be sustained and eventually de Gaulle forced him out. He retired in 1944 and died in 1949.

Giraud, (left) Roosevelt, de Gaulle and Churchill at the Casablanca Conference January 1943

Escape From the Japanese

Chapter 20

December 8 1941

Phillipines

Within ten hours of the massive attack on Pearl Harbour the Japanese embarked on an intensive aerial bombing campaign on Manila followed by a land invasion by ground troops. General Douglas MacArthur was in command of the American and Filipino troops charged with defending the archipelago, he had been recalled into active duty earlier in the year and was designated commander of the United States Armed Forces in the Asia/Pacific region.

The Japanese attack rendered his aircraft useless and the naval force assigned to protect the islands was withdrawn due to the attack on Pearl Harbour. He knew he had no chance of receiving reinforcements; therefore he and his troops withdrew to the Bataan Peninsula and Corregidor an island at the entrance to Manila Bay.

Manila was effectively handed over to the Japanese on 2 January 1942 to prevent its complete destruction.

The U.S. and Filipino forces continued to defend until surrender was negotiated in April 1942. Over eighty thousand POWs were taken into custody.

There began one of the most disgraceful episodes in modern warfare – the Bataan Death March.

Approximately seventy five thousand American and Filipino prisoners of war plus many Filipino citizens were assembled by their Japanese masters to embark on the Bataan Death Match. It is estimated over ten thousand didn't make it to the end dying from disease, starvation, beatings and all too often a Japanese sword or bayonet.

No matter what the prisoner's condition if they straggled behind they were murdered.

A favourite past time of the tank and truck drivers was to run over prisoners who had fallen to the ground from exhaustion.

The temperature hovered over thirty-five degrees with the humidity in the high nineties the heat together with the constant clouds of dust had the POW's craving for water. The route was dotted with artesian wells but the Japanese would not allow the prisoners to use them. If a prisoner was found drinking from a well he was either shot or beheaded. The only water the men were allowed was from the filthy carabao wallows used by the water buffalo. Dysentery was rampant. No food was given to the prisoners over the first three days of the march; finally, each man received a small ball of rice.

As the march was nearing its end about fifteen hundred men were jammed into large tin shed where the temperature rose to over forty degrees Celsius. There was one water tap, as a consequence many died while many others lost their minds.

The POWs finally reached their destination, Camp O'Donnell a former Filipino army camp north of Manila. If the prisoners thought things could only get better they were mistaken. The Japanese guards practiced the same level of barbaric cruelty as they did on the march. In the first two months at the camp sixteen hundred Americans and sixteen thousand Filipinos died of starvation, disease or beatings by the guards. Many were executed in front of their comrades.

After a couple of months some prisoners were moved to another camp, Cabanatuan, included in the group was Sam Grashio a pilot and his Wing Commander Ed Dyess.

Cabanatuan was not an improvement over O'Donnell the rations were just as meagre and the guards were just as cruel.

Sam and Ed survived the prison but many didn't. After four months they, and another one thousand POWs who were judged fit to work were sent to Dravo on the southern island of Mindanao. The prisoners were put to work farming, logging and other forms of manual work. The work was hard but the living conditions were an improvement on the previous two prisons. Despite the easing of the punishment and better conditions only half the prisoners were in a fit state to work six months after arriving at Davao.

Originally part of the Philippine prison system, Dravo was a maximum-security prison along the lines of France's Devil's Island but instead of water, Dravo's barrier was an impenetrable malaria-infested swamp containing wild natives, poisonous snakes and crocodiles. Dravo was situated within about one hundred and forty miles of arable land possessing fruit and nut orchards, vegetable and grain fields, and a mahogany forest worked by the prisoners. Upon conquering the Philippines, the Japanese Army took the prison to house POWs.

Dravo Prison Philippines

The Japanese had every reason to believe escape was impossible. In the ten years of Dravos existence, no prisoner had ever escaped. In addition, roughly thirteen hundred miles of ocean separated the POWs from nearest allied country, Australia. But escape is exactly what these ten men had in mind. Initially there were two independent escape teams, one led by McCoy and the other by the Marines. They learned of each other's plans and joined forces. From the middle of February to the end of March 1943, and with the help of a couple of sympathetic Filipino nationals, the men secretly smuggled out the items they'd need and buried them at the agreed jump-off site. No one else in the camp knew of their plan, secrecy was essential.

On Sunday morning, April 4, with musette bags filled with last-minute items slung over their shoulders, the men assembled to take part in their work details. As a guard checked them off on a blackboard, the men marched through the gate, ostensibly on their way to their assigned field of work.

As they did so, Frank Carpenter, an officer friend of Mellnik's shouted out jokingly, 'Hey, Steve! Your toothbrush is sticking out of the back of your musette bag. Are you planning to escape?'

Mellnik ignored the comment. Though Carpenter didn't know it, that's exactly what the men were doing.

Thirty minutes later they rendezvoused at a plougher's shack where they had secretly hidden supplies. At 10:30am they met up with two Filipinos who had agreed to guide them through the impenetrable swamp around Dravo. The men began cutting through the thick vegetation with their machetes it was very slow going.

At 6:00 p.m. the POWs assembled for the evening roll call. The guards began counting something was wrong, they did a recount – then a third. Bafflement gave way to a stunning realization. The unthinkable had happened – ten American POWs had escaped!

The Japanese commander was furious threatening the POWs who had shared a barracks with the escapees with death. The guards beat the camp commander and the barracks leaders in a vain attempt to extract information. They all knew nothing.

The Davao escapees from left to right, Maj. Steve Mellnik, Lt. Cmdr. "Chick" Parsons, Lt. Cmdr. Melvyn McCoy, Capt. Ed Dyess and Capt. Charley Smith

Inside each Daveo barracks, 150 to 200 POWs were sardined into 15-foot intervals of space called "bays." There were approximately 16 bays per barracks, eight on each side.

The first two days in the swamp was hell for the escapees their strength was much diminished. Despite having a compass, initially they got lost and found themselves going in circles. Better progress was made when they worked out a relay system where two men would hack away at the underbrush with bolos before being relieved. Compass readings taken at regular intervals ensured they maintained a north-easterly course.

On their second day of freedom, as evening approached, the morale of some of the exhausted men, some sick some delirious, collapsed. Dyess, as one of the original instigators of the escape, knew he should say something to improve the morale of the men, but felt Sam Grashio would be the better person as he was the most religious member of the group. Grashio, a Catholic, went to his knees and began reciting the "Memorare," a prayer to the Virgin Mary, pausing after each sentence, allowing the others to repeat it:

Remember, O most gracious Virgin Mary, never was it known that anyone who fled to your protection or sought your intercession was left unaided. Inspired by this confidence I fly unto you O Virgin of virgins, my Mother; to you I come, before you I stand, sinful and sorrowful. O Mother of the Word Incarnate, despise not my petitions, but in your mercy and kindness, hear and answer me. Amen."

Grashio's words had the desired effect. None of the escapees would ever be able to explain just what had happened that night – but Grashio knew.

'I thought a miracle had occurred,' he would say. 'I felt now that God would save us.'"

Four days later, they arrived at the village of Lungaog where they were greeted by Filipino guerrillas who agreed to help them get to Australia. The Filipinos guided them on a three hundred mile journey to a point where they could rendezvous with an Australian submarine and taken back to the Australian mainland and safety. The reception they received along the way was tremendous they were treated like celebrities

Grashio recalled 'After 12 months of brutality, starvation, and degradation, an abrupt change to such hospitality left us midway between tears of gratitude and utter bewilderment.'

In Australia, Dyess, McCoy, and Mellnik were presented to Commander General MacArthur who awarded them the Distinguished Service Cross.

Newspaper reports throughout America detailed the horrors of the Bataan Death March and how the Japanese ill-treated their POWs. When the USS *Missouri* was launched the President's daughter remarked.

'May this great ship be an avenger to the barbarians who wantonly slaughtered the heroes of Bataan.'

Miss Margaret Truman Launching the *USS Missouri*

The Rising Sun

The Cowra Mass Breakout

Chapter 21

Japan murdered approximately five million foreign civilians and POWs during the years 1937 to 1945. Add to that the hundreds of thousands who died from beatings, starvation and disease in the camps.

Many thousands of women and girls were raped and murdered particularly in Nanking China. Thousands more were forced into sexual slavery as "comfort women" in army brothels.

Finally, we cannot forget the terrible fate of hundreds of prisoners of war who were murdered by the Japanese Army's infamous Unit 731 in the course of horrible biological experiments.

The Japanese campaign in the Pacific was brutal and savage which the Western World could not and does not comprehend.

The order by the Japanese Army to the civilian population of the island of Saipan to kill themselves and their children rather than endure the shame of being captured underlays the Japanese Psyche. Unable to reach the Japanese villagers in time to stop this atrocity, American marines could only watch as hundreds of Japanese mothers threw their children off a cliff onto the coral below and then followed them. These child murders and civilian suicides were praised and encouraged back in Japan.

In 1942 on the Kokoda Track the Japanese and Australian forces fought a bloody battle in atrocious conditions. Not only did the Japanese murder all the Australian Diggers captured they compounded this horror by killing and eating wounded Australian soldiers.

Obviously the Japanese Government did not recognize "The Geneva Convention"

The Australians strictly observed the Geneva Convention regarding POWs.

Three years after Japan began the war in the Pacific there were two thousand two hundred and twenty three Japanese prisoners of war held captive in Australia

The POWs were well fed, given decent medical attention, and encouraged to partake in daily exercise. In winter, extra blankets and warm underwear was issued to the POWs. Under these conditions general health improved amongst the Japanese POWs. Many had been captured in New Guinea where the Japanese army had been decimated by tropical disease and weakened by starvation. Of the twenty one thousand Australian POWs captive under the care of Japan during the Second World War most were malnourished and worked to exhaustion. Eight thousand two hundred and ninety six Diggers died in captivity.

It was not the Japanese mentality to surrender; they found such an act to be humiliating and cowardly. When the Australian forces captured many Japanese soldiers in New Guinea the POWs often gave false names so that their families would presume them dead. They were shipped back to Australia where the majority were imprisoned at Cowra in New South Wales.

Cowra also imprisoned Italian POWs captured in the Middle East. The Japanese prisoners were housed in B compound. The Australian guards were well aware of the discontent of the Japanese but were not concerned about a possible break out.

Cowra POW Camp

A break out from Cowra would be extremely difficult; the prisoners had no access to weapons. An escape would involve negotiating three barbed wire perimeter fences and metres of entangled barbed wire. Six guard towers, each about nine metres high, and regularly patrolled by armed guards, dominated the camp perimeter.

The camp authorities received word from a Korean prisoner that the Japanese were planning a mass breakout. This was of great concern, they knew the camp had become overcrowded and there was considerable unrest amongst the prisoners.

The army supplied Cowra with two Vickers machine guns and many more rifles and ammunition to try and avert trouble. However, the camp administration did not increase the number of guards or hut searches.

No breakout was attempted and things seemed to settle down then, in early August camp officials began to separate the B compound inmates by relocating the junior ranks to a camp at Hay in western New South Wales.

Having been informed of the prisoner transfer on 4th August, Sergeant Major Kanazawa, the commander of B compound called a meeting of the twenty hut leaders.

He asked the leaders to return to their huts and gauge the level of support for a mass breakout.

There was much debate amongst the prisoners and although it was not a majority decision, the outcome was to launch a mass escape.

The escape plan called for all injured or incapacitated prisoners to commit suicide; this would allow them to restore their honour.

It was also agreed that no civilian would be harmed.

A bugle blast at 2.00 am would signal the breakout and all the huts would be torched

The prisoners were armed with camp cutlery and baseball bats. They had protection against the barbed wire fences by wearing baseball mitts and using blankets.

Broadway

The prisoners planned to 'hit' the wire in four groups. Two groups would scale the outer three fences and negotiate the ten metres of entangled and concertina barbed wire which lay there. The other two groups would break into Broadway, so called because of its bright lights at night. One of these groups would attempt to link up with the Japanese officers in D compound, while the other would attack the outer gates and the Australian garrison, which lay beyond.

The war cries of one thousand Japanese prisoners of war soon woke the guards; as they scrambled out of their beds they could smell the putrid smoke from the huts.

The bright lights of Broadway were soon expired by a bullet hitting the main electricity line.

The two new Vickers machine guns were put to use firing into the first wave of escapees however, the two young privates operating them were overwhelmed by the weight of numbers and were killed. Private Jones, before he was bashed to death, hid the gunlocks making the Vickers useless. His quick thinking denied the Japanese taking command of the camp.

The other three groups broke through the barbed wire fences. The prisoners in Broadway came under Australian fire from both ends and were pinned down for several hours. The attempt to link up with the officers in D Compound failed.

By contrast, almost all of the Japanese who crossed the perimeter wire outside B Compound escaped to freedom. Three hundred and thirty were on the loose.

It took nine days to recover them some travelled as far as Eugowra, a distance of over fifty kilometres.

The Royal Australian Air Force, police, Australian Military Force trainees and members of the Australian Women's Battalion stationed at Cowra all assisted with the roundup operations. Many escapees chose to take their own lives rather than be recaptured. Two threw themselves under an oncoming train, while many hanged themselves. On their recapture, some pleaded to be shot. Others surrendered peacefully. Local civilians and several military personnel shot at least two prisoners.

Lieutenant Harry Doncaster became the only Australian killed in the roundup, when he was attacked and murdered by a Japanese prisoner eleven kilometres north of Cowra. In total, two hundred and thirty one Japanese soldiers and officers were killed. One Japanese officer and one hundred and seven other Japanese soldiers were wounded. Four Australians had died. Four others were injured. The leaders of the breakout had ordered that no civilians be harmed, and they were true to their word.

Mount Kenya Looks Nice

Chapter 22

In January 1943, a group of Italian Prisoners of War escaped from POW Camp 354 in Nanyuki in Kenya. The three prisoners, Felice Benuzzi, Dr. Giovanni Balletto and Vincenzo Arsotti escaped from prison, went on a three-week adventure, and then returned giving themselves up to the prison commandant.

Felice Benuzzi was a man who didn't like being bored and he found the boredom of prison life suffocating. Felice would look out of the prison compound to the imposing site of Mt Kenya rising into the clouds; he often thought how wonderful it would be to climb the magnificent peak. One morning, a cathartic moment hit him.

'Why not break out of this place and climb the mountain.'

Benuzzi approached a fellow prisoner, a professional mountaineer, with the idea of escaping not to Italy but to climb Mount Kenya just for something exciting to do.

The mountaineer scoffed at the idea, telling Felice he was crazy. He pointed out that without the right climbing equipment and clothing he would surely die. Benuzzi was a very resourceful individual and was sure he would be able to manufacture the right equipment from bits and pieces he could steal from the kitchen.

He decided to make an approach to two friends, Dr. Giovanni ('Giuàn') Balletto and Vincenzo ('Enzo') Arsotti, a sailor. Benuzzi figured a doctor on the climb could be useful and a sailor should be resourceful. The two friends agreed to go.

On the 24th January, the three adventurers broke out of the British prison and began what would be an eighteen-day odyssey.

The only map they had of the mountain was on the label of an OXO tin. Enzo fell sick at the base of the mountain. He pushed on until he was too ill to go any further. The relentless Benuzzi and Giuàn continued their trek, reaching the high point of about 5000 meters on the North West ridge. They planted the Italian flag and left a message-bottle on Point Lenana.

They descended the mountain without incident; all three then broke back into the prison, amazing the camp commandant. His initial punishment was to impose solitary confinement for twenty-eight days but he commuted the sentence to seven days for such a sporting effort. All three mountaineers returned to Italy after the war.

Mount Kenya

Dammed Yankees

Chapter 23

America, the home of the brave, baseball and hotdogs had been at war for three years and in that time had established over five hundred POW camps across the land.

Four hundred thousand German POWs were transported to the United States during World War II. Like their Allied counterparts in German POW camps they believed it was their duty to escape. There were over two thousand individual attempts by the Germans to flee their camps. Prisoners scaled fences, smuggled themselves out in or under trucks or jeeps, passed through the gate in makeshift GI uniforms. They cut the barbed wire or tunnelled under it they even went out with work details and simply walked away. Their motives ranged from trying to find their way back to Germany (which none ever did) to merely enjoying a few hours, days, or weeks of freedom.

One particular camp, Papago Park in Arizona, housed more than three thousand German naval officers and sailors. To date it had been a very difficult camp to manage with attempted escapes and a lack of discipline being a major problem.

Towards the end of 1944 things seemed to change especially in compound 1A where the U-Boat commanders and crews were kept.

207

They had been the worst offenders now their compound was neat and tidy and the prisoners seemed more content and in good spirits. The guards were amazed and delighted with the change of attitude. Could these troublemakers be the same men who were now tending flowerbeds and playing sports including volleyball on the court they had constructed themselves?

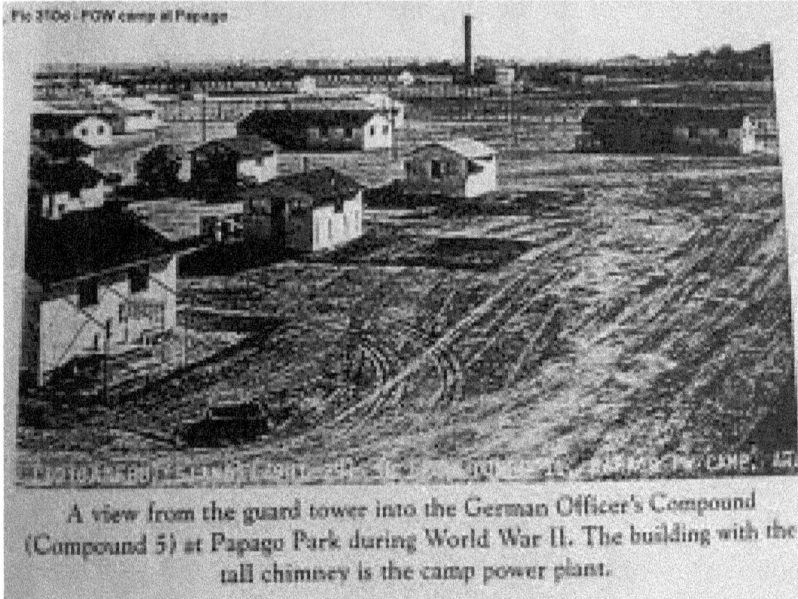

A view from the guard tower into the German Officer's Compound (Compound 5) at Papago Park during World War II. The building with the tall chimney is the camp power plant.

The prisoners were so proud of the volleyball court they groomed the surface several times a day. The guards put this fastidious behaviour down to German efficiency.

Captain Parshall an experienced camp official pointed out that there was a spot in Compound 1 that could not be seen from the guard towers.

'Those Germans were a fine bunch of men, smart as hell," he said later.

'It made no sense to put the smartest of them in Compound 1. I knew they would discover that blind spot.'

There was in fact a blind spot in Compound One that could not be seen from the guard towers. This would be a great spot to begin a tunnel.

The Geneva Convention exempted officers and NCOs from work detail, allowing them to sleep late and spend their days plotting ways to get beyond the wire.

Lieutenant Wolfgang Clarus, who had been captured in North Africa recalled.

'You stare at that fence for hours on end, try to think of everything and anything that can be done, and finally realize there are only three possibilities: go through it, fly over it, or dig under it.'

The officers in Compound 1A decided that an escape should be attempted and the logical method would be to dig a tunnel. A committee was established to manage the dig and tunnelling began in September 1944.

In September 1944 the digging began under the management of four officers, all U- boat captains, including Fritz Guggenberger, who had been personally decorated by Hitler for the exploits of his U Boat.

'The tunnel became a kind of all-consuming sport. We lived, ate, slept, talked, whispered, dreamed 'tunnel' and thought of little else for weeks on end.' Recounted Guggenberger.

Utilizing the blind spot the men chose the entrance shaft location three and a half feet from the bathhouse, which was the closest building to the perimeter fence.

A board was loosened on the side of the bathhouse creating a passageway and a coal box was moved to conceal the entrance to the tunnel.

The modus operand was the officers and men would enter the bathhouse to shower or wash their dirty clothes. Once inside they would slip down into the tunnel's six-foot deep vertical entrance shaft and begin their shift.

Three groups of three men worked ninety-minute shifts during the night, one man digging with a coal shovel and small pick, the second lifting soil in a bucket to the third man topside, who also served as the lookout.

As is always the case with digging illicit tunnels the major problem is getting rid of the dirt without drawing attention to yourself or the dirt itself.

At Papago they created a dedicated group to distribute the dirt the day after the dig.

They flushed it down toilets, stored it in attics, or let it slip through holes in their pockets onto the new flowerbeds. As the tunnel progressed, a small cart was fashioned out of a shower stall base to haul the dirt back to the entrance.

Soil piled up at such an alarming rate that a new means for getting rid of it had to be found. A captain in the group suggested they request a volleyball court be constructed, as a healthy way to keep the men occupied in the compound. The Americans thought that was a splendid idea and gave the go ahead. The ground they were to use was very rocky and uneven so it had to be levelled. The prisoners became very enthusiastic spreading the soil from the tunnels using rakes and shovels supplied by their captors.

A Colonel visiting the camp to inspect security declared 'this camp need never worry about prisoners digging out: the soil is as hard as a rock. He was standing right atop the concealed tunnel entrance at that moment

By their calculations the tunnel needed to be one hundred and seventy eight feet long enabling the tunnel to reach an electric light pole in a clump of bushes. This would route the tunnel under two fences and a patrol road.

Food provisions were going to be critical their main staple was to be breadcrumbs mixed with milk and water. Not very appetising but would fill their stomachs and it would be easy to carry.

The forgers were able to produce passports and identity papers from various odd and sods found around the camp including photos taken by the Americans and sent back to Germany to prove how well they treated German POWs.

On December 20 the tunnel had reached the desired length; to ensure they would exit at the electricity pole Guggenberger pushed a fire poker through earth. Prisoners in the compound could see that it was close to the pole, elation spread through the compound.

The escapees were ready to depart on the evening of 23 December. It had been arranged that their neighbours in Compound 1B would create plenty of noise. They certainly did, they drank homemade schnapps sang German songs and had a good old time.

Under cover of this diversion, the escape began through the bathhouse. The escapers proceeded in ten teams of two or three men each, some carrying packs laden with spare clothing, breadcrumbs and other food. Other teams carried medical supplies, maps and cigarettes. Shortly before nine o'clock in the evening, the first team, Quaet-Faslem and Guggenberger descended the entrance ladder and began struggling through the tunnel on elbows, stomach, and knees, pushing their packs ahead of them.

The journey took a little more than forty minutes. Guggenberger climbed the exit ladder and cautiously lifted the cover. A light rain was falling as he and his companion emerged into a clump of bushes and dashed down into the waist-deep ice-cold water of the nearby Crosscut Canal. By 2:30 a.m. all twenty-five prisoners; twelve officers and thirteen enlisted men had exited the tunnel and were making their way through a hard rain outside the wire of Papago Park. Colleagues who stayed behind closed up both ends of the tunnel.

The agreed plan was only to travel under cover of darkness avoiding trains or buses. Some hoped to cross into Mexico where they knew German sympathisers and hoped they would be assisted in getting back to Germany.

They all knew in their heart of hearts their chance of returning to Germany was very slim.

In the meantime they revelled in being free on Christmas Eve.

Some found stables where they rested amongst the bales of hay and ate their Christmas Eve meal of breadcrumbs. Others found abandoned shacks where they could eat and play "Silent Night" on the harmonica and others kept going right through the night.

On Sunday afternoon, Christmas Day, the Americans were due to conduct the head count. The German officers remaining demanded an officer, not a Sergent, conduct the rollcall. This delayed things somewhat.

Therefore, it wasn't until 7pm before the camp administration became aware of a mass break out.

It was about 7.30pm when Parshall was certain that a large group of prisoners were missing. He telephoned the FBI to report names and descriptions of the escapees. While he was still on that call, another telephone rang. It was the sheriff in Phoenix reporting they had an escaped POW in custody. Herbert Fuchs, a twenty-two-year-old U-boat crewman, had quickly grown tired of being wet, cold, and hungry and hitch hiked a ride to the sheriff's office. Soon after a Tempe woman called to say that two escapees had knocked on her door and surrendered; the telephone rang again, a man reported that two hungry and cold POWs had turned themselves in.

The Sheriff took one more call on Christmas Eve from Tempe railroad station informing him that another escapee had been arrested. This was Helmut Gugger a Swiss national who had been drafted into the German navy. Gugger revealed to the Americans the existence of the still-hidden tunnel the following day.

With a number of escapees already in custody authorities launched what the Phoenix Gazette headlined as "the greatest manhunt in Arizona history." Soldiers, FBI agents, sheriff's deputies, police, border patrol, and customs agents all joined the search for the nineteen German escapees still at large. Ranchers and Indian scouts attracted by the $25 reward carried mug shots of the escapees.

214

Captured German POWs

'We didn't think we were that important.' Guggenberger remarked later.

J. Edgar Hoover, director of the FBI, repeatedly warned the American public about the dangers posed by escaped German prisoners. In reality, there was not a single recorded instance of sabotage or assault on an American citizen by an escaped POW. Any crimes committed were typically the theft of an automobile or of clothing needed for the getaway.

After Christmas, most of the remaining nineteen prisoners moved south travelling under cover of darkness. Capture was a possibility at any moment; they were also cognisant of the fact that no fewer than fifty-six escaped German POWs were shot to death while escaping

Over the next fourteen days the German escapees either handed themselves in or were captured.

Their great escape was over except for the punishment, which turned out to be surprisingly light. Despite the egregious lapses in security, no American officer or guard was court-martialled. Some of the escapees half-expected to be shot however, they were merely put on bread and water for every day they were absent from camp.

Clarus said of the tunnel: "Conceiving of it, digging it, getting out, getting back, telling about our adventures, finding out what happened to the others...why, it covered a year or more and was our great recreation. It kept our spirits up even as Germany was being crushed and we worried about our parents and our families."

Germany to Vietnam

Chapter 24

Dieter Dengler was born May 22, 1938 and grew up in the small town of Wildberg, in the Black Forest region of the German state of Baden-Württemberg. Dieter never knew his father he had been killed in the Second World War; nevertheless he had a good family life despite the poor living conditions they all had to endure.

Dieter was very close to his Mother and brothers and they all worked together to survive life in post war Germany.

His grandfather was an avid opponent of Hitler's National Socialism and showed great strength in not voting for the Nazis in the elections. Dieter credited his grandfather's resolve in being the inspiration he needed in later life.

Dieter's first experience with aircraft was when he witnessed Allied aircraft bombing his hometown. From that moment, he wanted to be a pilot.

He grew up in extreme poverty, as a result he and his brothers discovered ways to keep the family fed and sheltered. They would go into bombed-out buildings, tear off wallpaper, and bring it to his mother to boil for a meal. Apparently, some nutrients remained in the wallpaper paste. When the Moroccans, who occupied the area, would slaughter sheep for their meals, Dieter would sneak over to their lodgings to take the scraps and parts they wouldn't eat. His mother was very inventive in the ways she could make a tasty meal. Dieter was also the first in his town to have a bicycle, building it himself by scavenging from dumps. He was apprenticed to a blacksmith at the age of fourteen, the blacksmith was a very hard taskmaster and beatings were a regular occurrence. Later in life, Dieter actually acknowledged his master for his disciplined training; it helped him become more capable, self-reliant, and tough enough to survive almost anything.

After seeing a recruitment advertisement in an American magazine looking for pilots, he decided to go to the United States.

The one thing that stopped him from going was lack of funds, he had to find a way to earn enough money to pay for his passage. He decided to salvage brass and other metals and sell them on the open market. This venture proved to be very successful and by the time he turned eighteen he had saved enough to sail to America.

Dieter made his way to Hamburg by hitching rides and walking departing for America and a new life. His final port was New York, a city that filled him with wonderment and awe.

He had nowhere to stay so he made the streets of Manhattan his home until he discovered the Air Force recruitment centre he applied and was accepted into the air force in 1957. Dieter was excited about the prospect of becoming a fighter pilot his lifetime ambition. He attended basic training in Texas and was assigned to work as a motor mechanic in the motor pool, hardly a dream fulfilled.

He took and passed the test to become an aviation cadet but his enlistment expired before he was selected for pilot training.

After his discharge, Dieter joined his brother working in a bakery shop near San Francisco he enrolled in the San Francisco City College passing his final year exams he then transferred to the College of San Mateo where he studied aeronautics. After graduating from college two years of college, he applied for the US Navy aviation cadet program and was accepted.

Dieter was determined to become a pilot. In his inaugural flight at flight training the instructor told Dieter that if he became airsick and vomited in the cockpit, he would receive a "down" on his record. He knew he was only allowed three downs before he received a fail. As Dieter expected, the instructor took the plane through spins and loops, causing Dieter to become dizzy and disoriented. Knowing he was about to vomit and not wanting to receive a down, Dieter took off his boot, threw up into it, and put it back on. At the end of the flight, the instructor checked the cockpit but couldn't find any evidence of vomit. Dieter still had a clean slate.

After his completion of flight training, he was assigned to Naval Air Station Corpus Christi, Texas for training to become an attack pilot in the Douglas AD Skyraider.

Douglas AD Skyraider

He joined his squadron, VA-145 while they were on shore duty at Naval Air Station Alameda, California. In 1965 the squadron joined the carrier *USS Ranger*

USS Ranger

In December the carrier set sail for the coast of Vietnam. He was stationed initially at Dixie Station off South Vietnam, and then moved north to Yankee Station for operations against North Vietnam. Life was about to change for Dieter.

Welcome to the Hanoi Hilton

Chapter 25

On February 1, 1966, the day after the carrier *Ranger* began flying missions from Yankee Station, Lieutenant Junior Dengler launched from the carrier with three other aircraft on an interdiction mission against a truck convoy that had been reported leaving North Vietnam. Thunderstorms forced the pilots to divert to their secondary target, a road intersection located west of the Mu Gia Pass in Laos. At the time, U.S. air operations in Laos were classified "secret." Visibility was poor due to smoke plumes emanating from burning fields. The flight formation lost site of each other Dengler was hit by anti-aircraft fire.

'There was a large explosion on my right side.' He remembered

'The airplane seemed to cartwheel through the sky in slow motion. There were more explosions yet, I was still able to guide the plane into a clearing in Laos.

Many times, people have asked me if I was afraid. Just before dying, there is no more fear. I felt I was floating.'

Thrown over thirty metres from the plane in a crash-landing, Dengler lay unconscious for a few minutes before making his way into the jungle to hide.

His squadron leader hoped to God that the young pilot would be rescued.

Dieter had earned himself a tough reputation while attending the navy survival school. He had escaped from a mock-POW camp run by SERE instructors and Marine guards twice, he had also set a record as the only student to actually gain weight during the course. His childhood experiences enabled him to eat whatever he could scavenge including the scraps the course instructors threw in the garbage.

Dieter's radio and survival kit were destroyed as a result of the crash landing; he really was on his own in enemy territory.

He only lasted a day before being discovered by the Pathet Lao, the Laotian allies of the Viet Cong.

He knew life was not going to be easy from then on; they tied his hands and marched him through the dense jungle

At night, he was tied spread-eagled on the ground to four stakes this not only prohibited him from escaping it prohibited him from getting any sleep. In the mornings, his face would be so swollen from mosquito bites he was unable to see clearly

He took an opportunity to escape into the jungle but it was a short-lived freedom, he was recaptured and subjected to a range of tortures.

He was hung upside down by his ankles with a nest of fierce ants covering his face eventually he would lose consciousness.

At night, they suspended him in a freezing well, he knew if he fell asleep he would drown.

Other times, he was dragged by water buffalo through villages, his guards laughing as they goaded both he and the animal with a whip.

Bloodied and almost broken, he was asked by Pathet Lao officers to sign a document condemning America, he refused, so the torture intensified. Tiny wedges of bamboo were inserted under his fingernails and into incisions on his body to grow and fester.

After some weeks, Dengler was handed over to the Viet Cong. As they marched him through a village, a man slipped Dieters's engagement ring from his finger. He complained to his guards. They found the culprit, summarily chopped off his finger with a machete and threw the finger aside once the ring was retrieved. Dieter was horrified. 'I realised right there and then that you didn't fool around with the Viet Cong. He said.

Dengler was eventually brought to a prison camp near the village of Par Kung where he met several other POWs.

They were:

Pisidhi Indradat (Thai)

Prasit Promsuwan (Thai)

Prasit Thanee (Thai)

Y.C. To (Chinese)

Duane W. Martin (American)

Eugene DeBruin (American)

Apart for Martin, an air force helicopter pilot who had been shot down in North Vietnam nearly a year before, the other prisoners were civilians employed by Air America, a civilian airline owned by the Central Intelligence Agency. The civilians had been in Pathet Lao hands for over two and a half years when Dengler joined them.

He had hoped he would be joining a group of pilots all plotting an escape; a bit like Douglas Bader and his comrades in World War Two.

What he saw horrified him, there was one man carrying his intestines cupped in his hands another had barely any teeth left, the few he had were badly ulcerated and extremely painful. He begged the other POWs to knock them out with a rock.

All the prisoners were in very bad shape Dieter knew he had to escape or he would end up like these poor fellows inside six months. He informed the other prisoners his intention to escape on his first day in the camp. They all suggested he wait until the monsoon season arrived ensuring he would always have access to fresh water. A few weeks after Dieter had arrived in the camp the Viet Cong moved them all to another camp just twenty kilometres away at Hoi Het.

The group split into camps, those who wanted to escape including Dieter, Martin and Prasit the others were opposed.

The food available became less and less the daily ration consisted of a cup of rice to be shared by all of them. The POWs occasionally caught a snake or a rat, which would be devoured by the prisoners; it was the only meat they could get.

Sleeping at night was difficult; the men were shackled together with their feet locked in foot blocks. They couldn't move, and together with the chronic dysentery most of them suffered they were forced to lie in their own excrement until being released in the morning.

Prasit Promsuwan, a Thai prisoner, overheard two guards discussing a plan to take the prisoners into the jungle and shoot them all. They were planning to make it look like an escape attempt then they could return home to their villages.

Prasit informed the other POWs as to what he had heard Dieter, was determined that he and the other men should escape as soon as possible. They lie bound in their shackles that night and devised a plan. At lunchtime the guards would lay down their weapons; this and the evening meal were the only times the guards were not armed. They agreed midday would be the best time to enact the plan so they could see their way when they entered the jungle. Dieter and another prisoner loosened the floorboards, which would enable them to squeeze through. The plan was to rush the guards seize their weapons and disappear into the jungle.

The Escape

June 26 1966

The group managed to break out of their manacles using sharpened bamboo to pick the locks the same method was used to free their feet. They all squeezed out between the floorboards and lay in wait for the guards to begin their lunch of rice and deer. They made their move running about five metres and grabbed the weapons including a M1 rifle Chinese automatic rifles and a sub machine gun. Dieter grabbed a AK47 just as five of the guards rushed him, he manage to shoot and kill three the other two escaped into the jungle

The seven prisoners split into three groups. DeBruin was originally supposed to go with Dieter and Martin however he decided to be with To to support his Chinese friend who was recovering from a fever and would be unable to keep up. They intended to get over the nearest ridge and wait for rescue. Dieter and Duane Martin decided to head for the Mekong River enabling them to escape to Thailand.

At last the two the two American airmen were free from the horrors of their camp however escape brought its own torments. Soon, the two men's feet were white and mangled from trekking through the dense jungle. This was similar to what the soldiers in the trenches during World War One called "trench feet".

They found the sole of an old tennis shoe, which they took turns wearing, strapping it onto a foot with rattan for a few hours respite.

They were able to make their way to a fast-flowing river.

'It was the highway to freedom.' Said Dengler,

'We knew it would flow into the Mekong River, which would take us over the border into Thailand and safety.'

The men built a raft from logs tied together with rattan and floated downstream encountering ferocious rapids along he way. At night they would tie the raft to a solid tree on the riverbank ensuring the raft wasn't swept away by the fast lowing torrent. He would wake to be greeted by hundreds of leeches sucking their much needed blood.

Dieter observed villages which looked familiar he was sure they had passed them days before; they had been going around in a circle this river would not take them to the Mekong and freedom.

They set up camp in an abandoned village where they found shelter from the incessant rain. Although Dieter and Duane had brought rice with them and were able to find other food they were still on the verge of starvation.

The two escapees were hoping to send a signal to an American C-130 which they had seen crossing over the village on a regular basis. Using the gunpowder from some carbine cartridges they had kept dry they were able to light a fire. They created torches from bamboo and bracken, they waved them when the C-130 flew above the village. To their delight the plane circled and dropped a couple of flares. They went to sleep that night feeling confident that a rescue mission would free them next morning. No such rescue happened.

When, next morning, they realised there would be no rescue both Dieter and Duane felt totally demoralised.

Duane convinced Dieter it was worth the risk to approach a nearby village, Akha to see if they could obtain some food. Dieter was reluctant but he would not abandon his friend, he agreed to go.

They entered the village and saw a young boy playing stick with his dog, the two men approached him smiling and holding out their hands. The boy turned and ran back to his home yelling "AMERICAN'. A male villager appeared almost immediately Dieter and Duane knelt down in supplication. The man swung a machete he was holding hitting Duane in the leg he struck again and Duane was decapitated.

Dieter quickly rose to his feet rushed towards the villager who turned and ran back into the village losing his rubber thongs in his mad rush to get help. Dieter picked up the thongs and ran back into the jungle before the other villagers confronted him.

The only highlight of his time in the jungle was befriending a bear it became his substitute dog following him wherever he went. It helped Dieter keep his sanity.

He was alone, staving and floating in and out of a hallucinatory state, he had little confidence that he would ever be rescued but he never gave up trying.

Dieter managed to evade the searchers who were searching for him escaping back into the jungle. He returned to the abandoned village that night when a C-130 came over Dieter set fire to the huts and burned the village down. The C-130 crew spotted the fires and dropped flares, but even though the crew reported their sighting when they returned to their base at Ubon, Thailand, the fires were not recognized by intelligence as having been a signal from a survivor.

When a rescue force again failed to materialize, Dieter decided to try and find one of the parachutes from a flare for use as a possible signal. He found one on a bush and placed it in his rucksack.

On July 20, 1966, after twenty-three days in the jungle, Dengler managed to signal an Air Force pilot with the parachute. Air Force Skyraiders from the 1st Air Commando Squadron happened to fly up the river where Dengler was located. Eugene Deatrick, the pilot of the lead plane and the squadron commander, spotted a flash of white while making a turn at the river's bend and came back and spotted a man waving something white. Deatrick and his wingman contacted rescue forces but were told to ignore the sighting, as no airmen were known to be down in the area. Deatrick persisted and eventually managed to convince the command and control centre to dispatch a rescue force. Fearing that Dengler might be a Viet Cong soldier, the helicopter crew restrained him when he was brought aboard.

Air Force Para-rescue specialist Michael Leonard stripped Dieter of his clothes, making sure he was not armed or in possession of a hand grenade. When questioned, Dieter told Leonard that he had escaped from a North Vietnamese POW camp two months earlier. Deatrick radioed the rescue helicopter crew to see if they could identify the person they had just hoisted up from the jungle. They reported that they had a man who claimed to be a downed Navy pilot who flew a Douglas A-1H Skyraider.

It wasn't until after he reached the hospital at Da Nang that Dieter's identity was confirmed. A dispute between the Air Force and the Navy developed over who should conduct his debriefing and recovery. In an apparent attempt to prevent the Air Force from embarrassing them in some way, the Navy sent a team of SEALs into the hospital to literally steal Dieter. He was brought out of the hospital in a covered gurney and rushed to the airfield, where he was placed aboard a Navy carrier delivery transport and flown to the *Ranger* where a welcoming party had been prepared. At night, however, he was tormented by awful dreams and had to be restrained.

Dieter's condition was such that the Navy decided to fly him back to the United States for treatment.

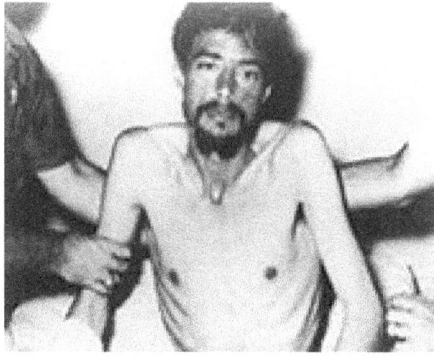

Photo taken of Dengler in the hospital after his rescue. At 175 cm Dengler weighed only 44.45 kilos.

'Seven of us escaped,' said Dengler. 'I was the only one who came out alive.'

With the exception of Indradat, who was recaptured and later rescued by Laotian troops, none of the other prisoners were ever seen again.

Heart of Glass

Chapter 26

Charles Glass

Charles Glass entered the lobby of the Summerland Hotel at five am on 18 August 1987 a free man. He had been kidnapped by Iranian backed Shi'ite terrorists while travelling in a motor vehicle with Ali Bey Osseiran, the son of Lebanon's defence minister, sixty-two days before. Putting his life on the line, Glass had been able to escape from his captors. What he didn't know at the time was that he was due to be released after a protracted negotiation between the Syrian Government and the terrorists.

Glass recounted his story:

'We were in a car on the coast highway going into Beirut. A green Mercedes turned left into the traffic ahead of us, blocking the road. Four men jumped out. I noticed a moment later that a similar thing happened just behind us. The men were all very young, in their late teens or early twenties, some with rifles, some with pistols. They told us to get out. One of them saw that I was looking for somewhere to run and shouted, in English, 'I will kill you.' It was chilling.

Two of them grabbed me and started pulling me toward the Mercedes. I was resisting. Someone came up behind and belted me with the butt of a rifle. It left my head a little bloody. They dragged me by my feet into their car and kept asking me who I was. I wouldn't tell them my nationality. My passport was in Ali's car, but my Lebanese press card, which they took from my back pocket, said I was American. I don't think they liked that too much. Or maybe they liked it a lot.

We went to an abandoned building where more men were waiting. They blindfolded and handcuffed us, and when it was very dark, they took us to an apartment. We weren't allowed to speak to each other, but they let us use the toilet. They gave us some sandwiches and fruit. With my fingernail, I carved onto an apricot HELP HOSTAGE, and when I went to the toilet I threw it out the window. I also took a cardboard centre from a toilet roll, cut my hand with a razor and, using a feather from a pillow, wrote a similar message that I threw out the window. They were long shots, but you never know. I said to myself on the first day that I was probably looking at a year or two. I was not happy at the prospect, but I wanted to prepare myself psychologically for the possibility.

After eight days I knew Ali and the driver were going to be released because the kidnappers came in and started telling them jokes. Two days after they had gone, the guards said, 'Get up and put on your clothes, you are going home to see your family.' I believed them. I was quite disappointed when I found myself being chained to a radiator in another apartment. Two days after that, I was moved again. The third apartment had a steel plate screwed over the window so that no light came in. The floor was bare except for a foam mattress on a piece of cardboard. There was a hole in the wall through which came the chain that was around my ankle.

I was never tortured, but there was mental abuse. I was forced at gunpoint to make a videotape, and I was told I'd never see my family again if I didn't. I had to write a statement [*in which Glass confessed to being a CIA operative*] in my own hand, but I didn't correct their grammar. I put on a Southern accent to show that I was in the southern suburbs. I tried to look terrified and sobbed to show I was under duress. At the end of the tape I changed my voice back to normal when I said to my family, 'I love you.'

They gave me my prayer book and three photographs of my family from my suitcase. These things sustained me. I prayed a lot, maybe six hours a day. I also constructed a novel in my mind and made a paper chess set and pretended to play my nine-year-old son, George. He always beat me.

I wrote messages in English, French and Arabic and pushed them through a vent in the bathroom wall. The guards found one and went berserk. They called their chief, who held up a grenade and said:

'We are not afraid to die. We are not afraid to kill you. If you make any more mistakes, you'll die.'

They moved me again the next night. They had no time to put up a metal sheet, so they just wedged a heavy wardrobe against the shutters leading to the balcony.'

Over the following week he gradually worked free of his chains, so that one night, when the guards slept in the next room, he was able to approach the shutters.

'I moved the wardrobe slowly, slowly outward, just enough to slip my body through to the balcony. It was seven stories up, and the roof was too high to reach, so I went through another door to a kitchen. To the left was the front door, the kind that could be opened only with the key, which, luckily, was in the lock. I slid back two dead bolts very quietly, then I locked the guards in.

I ran down the stairs and out on the street. It was after 1 a.m., and I didn't know where I was. I went into other apartment buildings looking for a name in English or French. They were all in Arabic, and many had little Khomeini pictures beside the bell, and I didn't think these were the right ones to wake up and ask for help. I then went to a bakery and asked for a telephone, and the two bakers started arguing about whether they had a telephone or not. Then a car drove up, and I asked the driver to take me to the Summerland Hotel. I told him I was Canadian, that my baby was sick and I had to fetch a doctor. It was only a five-minute drive. I entered the lobby and was greeted by the man on reception who knew me as a regular guest.

I wasn't a particularly devout person before, and I'm not born-again now. But I like to feel that God helped me.'

The Aftermath

Chapter 27

Douglas Bader

Bader was promoted to Group Captain following his return to the UK but left the Royal Air Force in 1946. He returned to his former employer where he eventually became managing director of a subsidiary, Shell Aircraft, serving until 1969 when he left to become a member of the Civil Aviation Authority Board.

Gunther Pluschow

After he left the Navy, Plüschow worked at various jobs before he was hired on the sailing vessel Parma, bound for South America. The ship took him around Cape Horn to Valdivia, Chile; he then travelled overland across Chile to Patagonia. On his return to Germany, he published Segelfahrt ins Wunderland ("Voyage to Wonderland"), which earned him enough for further explorations.

On November 27, 1927, Plüschow took the wooden two-masted cutter Feuerland to Punta Arenas, Chile. His engineer, Ernst Dreblow, brought his seaplane, a Heinkel HD 24 D-1313, aboard a steamer. By December 1928, the airplane had been fully assembled and the inaugural flight brought the first airmail from Puntas Arenas to Ushuaia, Argentina. In the months following, Plüschow and Dreblow were the first to explore by air the Cordillera Darwin, Cape Horn, the Southern Patagonian Ice Field, and the Torres del Paine of Patagonia. In 1929, Plüschow had to sell the Feuerland to obtain funds to return to Germany. There he published his explorations and photographs in a book, Silberkondor über Feuerland ("Silver Condor over Tierra del Fuego"), and a documentary film of the same name.

The following year, he returned to Patagonia to explore the Perito Moreno Glacier. There, both he and Dreblow were killed in fatal crash near the Brazo Rico, part of Lake Argentino, on January 28, 1931.

William Leefe Robinson

Robinson died on 31 December 1918 at the Stanmore home of his sister, the Baroness Heyking, from the effects of the Spanish flu pandemic to which his imprisonment had left him particularly susceptible. He was buried at All Saints' Churchyard Extension in Harrow Weald. A memorial to him was later erected near the spot where the airship crashed. This was renovated in 1986 and again in 2009, the latter occasion being to correct movement of the obelisk and surrounding footpath caused by subsidence.

An additional monument was erected in East Ridgeway, unveiled on 9 June 1921, and by a road named after him (Robinson Close) in Hornchurch, Essex on the site of the former Suttons Farm airfield. A short segment of a wartime newsreel survives although the location and date of the recorded event is unknown.

He was commemorated by the name of the local Miller & Carter steakhouse just south of the cemetery, the Leefe Robinson VC on the Uxbridge Road, Harrow Weald.

In April 2010, to celebrate the 100th anniversary of the Great Northern Route extension that connects Grange Park to Cuffley, the

First Capital Connect rail company named a Class 313 train Captain William Leefe Robinson VC.

Winston Churchill

In 1900, Churchill returned to England on the RMS Dunottar Castle, the same ship on which he had set sail for South Africa eight months earlier. He published "London to Ladysmith" and a second volume of Boer war experiences, "Ian Hamilton's March". Churchill stood again for parliament in Oldham in the general election of 1900 and won. After the 1900 general election, he embarked on a speaking tour of Britain followed by tours of the United States and Canada, earning in excess of £5,000.

In 1900, he retired from the regular army and in 1902 joined the Imperial Yeomanry, where he was commissioned as a Captain in the Queen's Own Oxfordshire Hussars on 4 January 1902. In that same year, he was initiated into Freemasonry at Studholme Lodge, he was promoted to Major and appointed to command of the Henley Squadron of the Queen's Own Oxfordshire Hussars. In September

1916, he transferred to the territorial reserves of officers, where he remained till retiring in 1924

In October 1911, Churchill was appointed First Lord of the Admiralty a position he held until May 1915. Churchill was removed from the Admiralty because of his incompetency in managing the disastrous Gallipoli Campaign. He remained in the Cabinet for six months as Chancellor of the Duchy of Lancaster until the decision was made to evacuate the Gallipoli peninsular.

Neimeyer - Holzminden

Committed suicide soon after the Great War ended.

Frank Savicki

After his successful escape i.e. "Home Run" he returned to America and managed a pool hall for many years.

Willy Williams

Was murdered by Hitler's SS in a forest somewhere in Germany.

Horace Greasley

Horace returned to England.

Greasley had two children by his first wife Kathleen, Stephen and Lesley. He married his second wife Brenda in 1975 and moved to Spain where he remained until his death at the age of 91.

In spring of 2008, ghost-writer Ken Scott was introduced to Horace Greasley so, aged eighty-nine, he could finally have his World War II memoirs recorded. Scott stated that he only acted as Horace's fingers to type the book as Horace suffered from extreme arthritis. The book was finished and published by the end of 2008 by Libros.

Franz von Werra

On 25 October 1941 Von Werra took off in his new plane on a practice flight. He suffered engine failure and crashed into the sea north of Vlissingen and was killed. His body was never found.

Holzmiden

The barracks are still being used by the German Army.

A few notable POWs went on to very successful careers including:

JAMES WHALE - Hollywood Film Director

Englishman James developed a love of drama and theatre when he became involved in the Gaiety Theatre, an amateur theatre group formed by Holzminden prisoners to stave off boredom. He went on to distinguish himself as film and theatre director in Hollywood, directing over 23 films such as Frankenstein (1931), The Bride of Frankenstein (1935), the musical Showboat (1936) and The Man In The Iron Mask (1939).

HECTOR FRASER DOUGALL - Media Pioneer

Trench warfare prompted Canadian Expeditionary Force Lieutenant, Hector, to seek a commission in the Royal Flying Corps. Shot down over France, he was incarcerated at Holzminden in May 1918 but not before he made many colourful escape attempts. When the Holzminden camp was liberated in December 1918, Hector climbed to the top of the camp flagpole and captured the Prussian flag, which bore the State emblem of an eagle. When he returned to Canada, he remained close to his aviation passion -- flying in air shows, barnstorming and forming the Fort William Aero Club. He also co-formed the Dougall Motor Car Co., and later two radio stations and a CBC-affiliated television station.

SIDNEY STEWART HUME - Psychiatric Patient

Not all POW stories had a happy ending. Argentinian born Sidney, a spotter/observer in the Royal Flying Corps, was shot down over France in May 1917. He was incarcerated in a number of POW camps, where he was reportedly treated badly by his German captors, who he accused repeatedly of hypnotising him. The psychological anguish of his experiences -- real or imagined -- triggered a backward slide in to mental illness, which was to become Sidney's constant and tragic companion. Back in England after the war, he was diagnosed with delusionary insanity and shot dead an orderly whom he mistakenly believed to be a German spy. Sidney was to be tried for murder and was incarcerated in a psychiatric facility for the rest of his century-long life.

Colditz Castle

When the Second World War came to an end the land where Colditz was situated in Saxony was conceded to the Russians. The Communists began to impose their political agenda. Industry was nationalized and private property including land passed into state ownership.

In July 1945 large estate owners were expelled from the ancient state of Saxony. Families who had lived in the same house for six hundred years were given an hour to vacate. They were taken to holding camps including Colditz. Here they were imprisoned in quarters vacated just two months before by the Allied prisoners of war. Two families were allocated to one room. For the adults it was an uncertain time, but for the children the castle was a playground.

After the reunification of Germany in 1990 the castle lay dormant.

During 2006–07, the castle underwent a significant amount of refurbishment and restoration which was paid for by the state of Saxony. The castle walls were repainted to reflect the look of the castle pre World War II.

With renovations largely completed, the castle now includes both a museum conducting guided tours showing some of the escape tunnels built by prisoners of the Oflag during World War II. The chapel, although accessible to visitors, is in disrepair.

The outer courtyard and former German Kommandantur (guard quarters) have been converted into a youth hostel

Bibliography

Web Sites

Zeppelin Raiders – History of British Pilots who Shot Down German Airships in WW1
Captain William Leefe Robinson, V.C., Awarded the Victoria Cross – Worcestershire Regiment
Captain William Leefe Robinson, V.C., Taken Prisoner of War – Worcestershire Regiment
Inspired Ambitions: Early 1900's Photographs of Sexy Women
A book lifts the lid on the carnal comforts sought by First World War troops | World news | The Observer
WHO'S WHO
Escape From Germany – Neil Hanson – Google Books
Revealed: the Great Escape of 1918 | Art and design | The Observer
Untitled Normal Page
World War I 'Great Escape' plot revealed in new exhibition – Telegraph
Escape From Germany – Neil Hanson – Google Books
Prisoners of War in WW1
Mass escapes from German POW camps – Wikipedia, the free encyclopedia
Virtual Colditz – A Visual Tour of Colditz Castle
Disturbing the Bodies · Meanjin · Literacy in Australia · Melbourne University Publishing · Classic English Literature Books · Australian Literary Journals & Magazines
The role of Poperinge in World War I – by Jerome Carter – Helium
Poperinge and World War One
Colditz Castle – Wikipedia, the free encyclopedia
Attempts to escape Oflag IV-C – Wikipedia, the free encyclopedia
World War I Air Ace and Escape Artist
The Cowra Breakout
World War One Battlefields : Flanders: Poperinghe
True story of the Great Escape
WW1_dogs_pdf
World War 1 Dogs and Animals,animals used in ww1,animals of ww1,articles abo...les about ww1 pigeons,articles about ww1 elephants,articles about ww1 animals
Horace Greasley – Telegraph
Horace 'Jim' Greasley Official Site
I escaped from Auschwitz | World news | The Guardian
Escape attempt from Auschwitz–Birkenau! www.HolocaustResearchProject.org
Convert Words to Pages – Free Calculator (select font & size)
Norman Cross – Wikipedia, the free encyclopedia
King's Lynn – Friends of Norman Cross
Prisoners of war
Historical articles and illustrations » Blog Archive » Winston Churchill's lucky escape from the Boers
The Boer Wars – Personalities – Second Boer War – Sir Winston Churchill
Anglo Boer War website – Camps for Boers – Ceylon (Sri Lanka)
Franz von Werra – Wikipedia, the free encyclopedia
Oberleutnant Franz von Werra
Punic War POWs – Prisoners of War in Punic Wars
Prisoner of war – Wikipedia, the free encyclopedia
The Douglas Bader Foundation – » Sir Douglas Bader
The Not-So-Great Escape: German POWs in the U.S. during WWII
BBC News – Colditz escape: Tale of first British 'home run' revealed
Japanese war crimes – Wikipedia, the free encyclopedia

Books

Colditz   P R Reid

Escape From Germany   Neil Hanson

Gunther Pluschow   Anton Rippon

248